In this fascinating book, Kirk Schneider—who has spent a distinguished career defending the core values of psychotherapists against dehumanizing pressures from an increasingly consumeristic, objectifying environment—helps readers find ways to survive and flourish in our stressful world. Instead of trying to soothe our fears that much is out of kilter in contemporary life, he suggests that if we are not anxious *enough* about the right problems, we risk being unequipped to address them. **This provocative, brilliant, and paradoxically comforting book belongs in the library of anyone who cares about the fate of humanity.**

Nancy McWilliams, PhD, ABPP, Distinguished Affiliate Faculty, Rutgers Graduate School of Applied and Professional Psychology, author of *Psychoanalytic Diagnosis and Psychoanalytic Psychotherapy*

Life-Enhancing Anxiety challenges us to rethink our understanding of anxiety as something to be avoided or managed at all costs. Instead, Schneider urges us to consider the many ways this basic human emotion can help us grow, more fully engage with existence, and transform ourselves in ways that lead to more fulfilling lives. In his view, anxiety is inherently tied to the experience of awe, a transformative experience that has become harder to come by in the increasingly regimented and standardized lives most people live. This is a provocative thesis that integrates ideas from previous existential thinkers, empirical research, Schneider's decades of experience as a psychotherapist, and his insightful contemplation of his own life trajectory. **It is a stimulating and rewarding read that will be of great value to psychotherapists, scientists, and lay people alike.**

Tom Pyszczynski, PhD, Distinguished Professor of Psychology, University of Colorado, Colorado Springs. Co-author of *The Worm at the Core: On the Role of Death in Life* with Jeff Greenberg & Sheldon Solomon

In a world where any signs of discomfort are met with harshness to the point of total loss of tolerance for ambiguity, uneasiness, and disputation; and resilience has become a teachable skill rather than a natural and acquired fruit of life, *Life-Enhancing Anxiety* is a breath of fresh air. Schneider puts forward a solid argument based on empirical evidence, years of clinical work, and personal experience to remind us of the necessity of recognizing anxiety as a life force. He invites us to reconsider the existential roots of anxiety as a powerful mobilizer and not a paralyzer. **The wisdom shared in this book should be enlightening for fellow mental health practitioners and their clients, community educators, and students.**

Dr. Sara Nasserzadeh, Co-Founder of Relationship Panoramic Inc. & Senior Advisor to the United Nations

In a world mired in anxiety and fear, Professor Kirk Schneider presents a ground-breaking analysis of anxiety while examining the deeply rooted existential nature of human disturbances. **Schneider beautifully and powerfully illustrates the inescapability of anxiety in the human condition and provides a rigorous model of psychological hardiness.** Schneider's life-enhancing anxiety goes beyond the reductionist models of anxiety and delves into the interplay of elements that create the anxiety-inducing paralysis in our social and cultural milieu. While celebrating the bridge between philosophy and psychology, Schneider elucidates the vitality of awe for a more transcendent, sagacious mode of being.

Sayyed Mohsen Fatemi, PhD, Adjunct Faculty, Department of Psychology, York University.
Author of *The Psychology of Inner Peace, Film Therapy*, and forthcoming, *Therapeutic Applications of Langerian Mindfulness*

One of the most common misconceptions about psychotherapy is that it helps us relieve anxiety. Yet, existentialist philosophers have always argued the contrary, that therapy should be employed to *promote* anxiety. **In this timely and radical study, Kirk Schneider, one of the world's leading existential therapists, once again regales us with his uncanny ability to ease us into truths that we all too often wish to avoid. In showing that anxiety is not our enemy but a friend that can potentially help us embrace life to the fullest, this remarkable book is destined to become a classic.**

M. Guy Thompson, PhD, Founder and Director, New School for Existential Psychoanalysis; author, *The Death of Desire: An Existential Study in Sanity and Madness; The Legacy of R. D. Laing: An Appraisal of his Contemporary Relevance*

In this expansive text, Kirk Schneider probes life's fundamental questions and takes the reader on a search for depth, meaning, connection, and love. He traverses key aspects of society and self to define what's needed to heal divides in our cultures, politics, relationships, and selves. **Drawing from our experiences with COVID, political divides, racial and economic injustice, armed conflicts at home and abroad, tensions over school curricula, climate change, and more, Schneider outlines how the psychology and science of anxiety are key to understanding and solving these problems. He even puts himself on the couch, with exquisite vulnerability.** In an adept interplay of our most personal engagements with our sociocultural surround, Schneider illuminates how we can live amidst paradox, embrace anxiety, and transform suffering into growth. **This is an essential read for those looking to understand our culture and our times and to create a life of deep meaning and purpose.**

Linda Michaels, PsyD, MBA, Chair and Co-Founder, Psychotherapy Action Network (PsiAN) Psychologist, Consulting Editor of *Psychoanalytic Inquiry*, and Fellow of the Lauder Institute Global MBA program

Schneider offers a vital solution to addressing the epidemic of life-destroying anxiety plaguing our patients and clients. We desperately need a bigger picture of allaying anxiety than conventional psychology, pharmaceuticals, and avoidance through addiction to technology. Cultivation of life-enhancing anxiety is the paradigm shift to cultivate the capacities of love, creativity, humility, wonder, and a sense of adventure toward living—what Schneider calls "awe"—in the midst of so many unknowns. **For humanity to thrive in our next chapter on Earth, we need this brilliant book to open a new door to embracing (and engaging with) Life-Enhancing Anxiety.**

Michael Amster, MD, coauthor of *The Power of Awe* and researcher at the UC Berkeley Greater Good Science Center

Life-Enhancing Anxiety: Key to a Sane World

Kirk J. Schneider, PhD

University
PROFESSORS PRESS

Colorado Springs, CO
www.universityprofessorspress.com

ISBN (Hardcover):   978-1-955737-19-7
ISBN (Paperback):   978-1-955737-18-0
ISBN (Ebook):   978-1-955737-20-3

University Professors Press
Colorado Springs, CO
www.universityprofessorspress.com

Cover Image by Ilene A. Serlin
Cover Design adapted by Laura Ross
Back cover photo by Jurate Raulinaitis

Dedication:
To Jurate, Benjamin, and Sarah

Table of Contents

Introduction

What the World Needs Now:
Life-Enhancing Anxiety

"Freedom and anxiety are two sides of the coin. There
is never one without the other."
— Rollo May (1981, p. 190)

It seems counterintuitive. Anxiety is going through the roof in our time,
and yet this book advances the notion that *there is not enough anxiety—*
at least of a certain kind. People are laboring in the thousands, maybe
millions, with anxiety disorders. There is a war going on in Ukraine,
authoritarianism is on the rise, and climatic disaster is upon us. These
crises are driven by as well as perpetrating anxiety; and yet this volume
raises the prospect that the crises are the result of *avoidance* of *a certain
type of* anxiety. I call this *life-enhancing* anxiety.[1]

As we will see, life-enhancing anxiety is the anxiety we must face to
prevent life-destroying anxiety. It is challenging and requires pluck. But
it also may just save us from the disastrous path with which we now
contend.

Anxiety is discomfort with the unknown. It is typified by muscular
tension, elevated pulse, and activated sweat glands. But it is also
characterized by a sense of excitement and discovery. In the
conventional view, so-called "normal" anxiety is mild to moderate
discomfort with the unknown. It is the tension or sweat we experience
when we are about to undergo an operation or be called in for a job
interview. "Neurotic anxiety" is an excessive or irrational discomfort
with the unknown. It is the intense discomfort some of us experience at
the sight of a spider, for example, or a person from a foreign country. In
either case, whether normal or neurotic, anxiety is experienced as one

---

[1] My gratitude goes to Robert Kramer for spontaneously coining the phrase "life-
enhancing anxiety" during a conversation we had about my development of this book.
The phrase has been used elsewhere but not precisely as I've defined it or within the
full scope of how I have applied it.

dimension—discomfort. The elements of excitement and wonder, on the other hand, are almost entirely lacking. Therefore, we need a bigger picture of anxiety than conventional psychology has thus far offered.

The chief question today is how do we view the unknown—and thus anxiety? Do we see it as a gateway and not merely an obstacle to human flourishing? Can we appreciate it for its full array of qualities—not merely those that deaden, block, and paralyze, but also those that enrich, deepen, and mobilize? Can we perceive it in its complexity, filled with sometime anguish but also with sometime energy, possibility? How do we view anxiety in the face of such anxiety-provoking challenges as COVID-19?

Despite what we indeed know about anxiety's multifacetedness (e.g., see van der Kolk, 2014), the facts are plain; we almost never talk about *"life-enhancing"* anxiety in our culture, or in cultures akin to ours that strive to eradicate anxiety.

What specifically do I mean by life-enhancing anxiety? I mean *anxiety that enables us to live with and make the best of the depth and mystery of existence.* I also mean the energizing lifestyles, encounters, and inquiries that lead to richer, more gratifying, more invigorated lives. Life-enhancing anxiety encompasses but goes beyond "post-traumatic growth." This is because life-enhancing anxiety addresses constructive responses not only to explicit trauma but also to the jolts and shocks of *everyday* life. Life-enhancing anxiety, in other words, addresses our capacity to grow from the ups and downs of life itself—and not just parts of life.

While life-enhancing anxiety can raise blood pressure and release stress hormones, it generally presents as a state of organismic flourishing, of intrigue and engagement with life, somewhere between normal and neurotic. This is why people of all kinds—be they meditators, inquirers, or just plain seekers of wisdom—tend to experience life-enhancing anxiety as a byproduct of full living rather than as an extraordinary response to an extraordinary event. But don't mistake this calm intensity for shallowness. To the contrary, it is more often a sign of depth, concerted reflection, and passionate concern for the health and well-being of all.

The under-appreciated reality is that life-enhancing anxiety is a necessary condition for presence, and *presence, or the holding and illuminating of that which is significant, alive, relevant,* may be one of the chief prerequisites to vital living (Bugental, 1987). The rudiments of presence begin at birth, and maybe before. They are our first contacts with objects and people who *differ* from us, and they challenge us at all levels. Specifically, they challenge us to both *assimilate*, that is integrate new experience into existing experiences (or frameworks) and to *accommodate* or find new frameworks to handle new experiences.

Thus, our first contact with touch, taste, smell, sound, sight, and imagination form the building blocks of presence, and challenge us to hone and refine presence. But that presence cannot be honed and refined if we aren't able to develop a tolerance for and eventually perhaps an intrigue with the state of arousal generated by experiences of difference. We call that arousal *anxiety*, and anxiety can only become "life-enhancing" if we can bolster our ability to assimilate and accommodate it.

How do we do this? While part of the answer resides with our temperament, the lion's share, I contend, derives from the parents and culture that raise us. Those who raise us, in other words, even in our prenatal environment, can have a profound impact on how we "hold" anxiety—how we assimilate and accommodate to differences from our tranquil state of unity (Piaget, 2006; Winnicott,1965). The hope, of course, is that those who raise us have also optimized capacities to hold difference and thus anxiety in their worlds. The hope also is that those caretakers can in turn transfer their capacities to manage differences to their newborn (or even prenatal) children. As we will see, this is a very subtle and complex process, and if not handled well—either by caretakers or the cultures from which they derive—we end up with appallingly disabled children who go on to be appallingly disabled (e.g., fearful, resentful and too often destructive) adults.

Hence the cultivation of presence is the beginning of cultivating life-enhancing anxiety; and the cultivation of life-enhancing anxiety opens the doorway to many gratifying experiences. Among these are the capacities to love, to imagine, to create, and to discover the humility and wonder, sense of adventure toward living that I call "awe" (Schneider, 2009).

Still, there are very few places in this world that seem conducive to maximizing life-enhancing anxiety. As I mentioned previously, many of the cultures we grow up in, particularly today, stress the eradication of anxiety, life-enhancing or not. Even when these cultures appear to amplify what might be called constructive anxiety—as purportedly occurs during dazzling displays of technology, thrilling athletic events, or high stakes business transactions—appearances are deceiving. Underlying these visceral thrills, many cultures still place a premium on *delimiting the more consequential anxieties* (e.g., those that pertain to the depth and mystery of existence). Among these more consequential anxieties are the cultivation of longer term, emotionally gratifying relationships; the struggle with climate change; the encounter with racial and political injustice, and the tangle with meaning and purpose in life.

Thus, many of our lives are either dominated by quick highs and vicarious thrills, or the eradication of anxiety altogether; but we miss contending with the really critical anxieties of thinking through personal and social problems and contributing to the longer-term betterment of humanity. This omission is pivotal because sooner or later it catches up with us and breaks out into epidemics of just what we were so fearful of in the first place: crippling, destabilizing anxiety! In short, anxiety is almost never seen as a gateway to human flourishing in power centers across the world. But these power centers pay a huge price for that one-sidedness—regimentation, shallowness, and ironically unintegrated, disabling anxiety.

To be sure, we've had some masterful counter-narratives to the above trends, but they are too often rarified, or seen as such by dominant powers. Taoism, for example, stresses the way of nature vs. the way of dogma. The South African philosophy of Ubuntu emphasizes acknowledging one another's unique and vulnerable humanity. The U.S. Constitution urges tolerance and equality under the law. The Islamic and Hebraic credos call for embracing the stranger. Many Native American sensibilities advise that we venerate the powers and mysteries of earth, and Hindu and Buddhist approaches plea for us to reconcile with impermanence. Yet to what degree have the power centers of the world—such as the Greco-Roman empire, Great Britain, Germany, China, Japan, Russia, and the United States (at least in their institutionalized forms)—really heeded these cries? How much have they *respected* them? Even more important, how much will the legacies these cultures have produced draw on the wisdom of the counter-narratives to inform our encroaching future? Our present stress on speed, instant results, and "anxiety-free" lifestyles does not bode well for the openness exhibited by the counter-narratives; nor does the prevailing view bode well for a sane and nuanced view of life, a life of wholeness and respect for other lives.

Let me be clear that I am not advocating a simplistic view of the counter narratives, but one that fully acknowledges life's ambiguities. Sometimes there are trends such as the expedient use of "mindfulness" or "spirituality" that profess to counter our efficiency-based world but end up fueling it through grandiose promises or cosmetic methods. These methods too often foster quick profits or fleeting highs, but they falter when it comes to our ability to live with and make the best of the depth and mystery of existence. I would say that this is the pivotal divide between forms of mindfulness and spirituality that acknowledge life's perplexities (e.g., see Batchelor, 1998 and Fatemi, 2021) and those that specialize in ploys.

Not since the warnings of such existential visionaries as Kierkegaard, Nietzsche, Sartre, and Tillich, or their successors Rank, May, Becker, Laing, and Foucault have we needed more desperately to come to grips with anxiety. For these thinkers, and in my own very personal experience, anxiety is assuredly two-edged. It is *both* an impediment to *and potentially* a signal of human flourishing; and its viability now is pivotal. Why? Because, again, unlike any other time in history we are in a position to virtually eradicate anxiety.

Think for example, of how many devices—drugs, games, phones— keep us occupied and quell our distress. Think of the 800-channel TVs, thousands of websites, plethora of sports and flood of entertainments that keep our uncomfortable conversations, as well as our inner thoughts, at bay. Consider how much of life can veer away from exploration, risk-taking, and person-to-person engagement.

On the other hand, anxieties are flaring up all around us, and we suppress them at our peril. We have a once-in-a-century pandemic that has claimed millions of lives and threatens millions more. In the United States we have wild fires in the West and mega-storms in the East; and in the North we've got melting ice-caps and rising seas. In short, we have a climatic and viral disaster on our hands and only a modest collective will to arrest them. We also have mass migrations and mass displacement of workers, mass alienation and mass disenfranchisement from historical norms, growing divisions among classes, races, and ideologies. We also have *lethal* divisions among classes, races, and ideologies. What does it take to slaughter innocent black people in a grocery store? What kind of mentality rears itself to kill 19 elementary school children in their classroom or 11 worshipers at a Pittsburgh Synagogue? Sure, mental disorder is an issue, but the hollow culture that nourishes it is just as much an issue, and not discussed nearly enough!

We also have a major war in Europe and growing prospects for more wars—not just culture wars but further and equally catastrophic wars over famine, water rights, medicines, and long bitter territorial disputes. And as if that were not enough, we continue to have the hydrogen bomb looming over us, coupled with tepid efforts to manage it. It is no wonder we make such massive efforts to stave off our anxiety. Our anxiety is (understandably!) *massive.*

The irony, however, is that it has been the very avoidance of our anxiety that has led to so many of the anxiety-provoking disasters we face, and for which we are now paying dearly.

Clearly then, we are at a crossroads. We've got more anxiety per capita, more dread of the unknown and its consequences than at perhaps any other time in history; and yet we also have the infrastructure, the technocratic and medical knowhow to steamroll that anxiety, or at least provide the illusion of such eradication, until all too predictably the illusion fails. Finally, we have the tools to face and work with our discomforts. Ideally, we can do this early on—from the start of life, for example; but more realistically from the start of our descent into quick fixes and dangerous distractions,

This book, accordingly, is a collection of essays that readmit anxiety into the heartbeat of life. Although Rollo May (1950) wrote a classic about anxiety and certainly spoke to the difficulties of his era, it is now time for a renewal of that inquiry. Each essay or chapter addresses a slightly different angle on the nature and implications of anxiety for our times, and each builds toward a reformation in our thinking about and, most important, engagement with life-enhancing anxiety. The stakes could not be higher.

Part 1

From Terror to Wonder to Awe:
A Path to Life-Enhancement

Overview

This section explores the nature and basis of life-enhancing anxiety. Through both professional and personal lenses, I elaborate fresh findings on the roots and impact of anxiety over the life span and, indeed, the history of humanity. I also cover the shift from a fear-based to an awe-based approach to life. The basic arc of this shift seems to follow a pattern: from terror and repulsion to "otherness" to intrigue, wonder, and ultimately awe toward "differences"—and toward all life. I define awe as the humility and wonder or sense of adventure toward living that epitomizes the value of life-enhancing anxiety.

Chapter 1

Unpacking Anxiety

Just how long have human beings suffered from and committed heinous acts because of anxiety? Quite possibly since we became human beings. In his riveting work *Sapiens*, Yuval Harari (2015) suggests that the avoidance of anxiety, which again is fear of the unknown, may have been responsible for the first genocide in human history. This arguably took place some 40,000 years ago when quite abruptly the Neanderthal lineage of humanity vanished, and the Homo sapiens lineage (our lineage today) replaced it.

This alleged "genocide" may have been the result of a very long struggle dating back to 125,000 years ago. This is when Neanderthals dominated the fertile terrains of the Middle East and parts of Europe and the Homo sapiens were confined to Africa with little or no ability to expand into superior Neanderthal lands (see Nicholas Longrich, 2020), But according to Harari, once the Homo sapiens achieved military superiority over the Neanderthals, wiping them out completely did not seem to be an inevitable outcome; nor did it seem necessary for the survival of Homo sapiens. Yet genocide may well have been what the Homo sapiens pursued (Harari, 2015, p. 18). Why?

In order to answer this question, we need to look beyond evolutionary psychology. This is because evolutionary psychology can explain the need for physical domination in the name of group or individual survival, but it has more difficulty explaining mass slaughter in the absence of the need for survival. There is an extra element here—beyond what the evolutionists call "signal anxiety"—which prepares organisms to either flee or fight. Genocide, whether it was perpetrated by the Homo sapiens or the Nazis does not seem to be explainable on purely physiological grounds: the grounds of physical survival. It may, however, be more explainable on psychological and symbolic grounds, grounds that point to threats to one's sense of self, one's cohesion, and even one's worthiness for life.

Our world is filled with these non-strictly physical threats today—threats to our cultural and racial identities, threats to our class and religious affiliations, threats to our national and political identities, even threats to our sense of self as worthy and deserving human beings. What is becoming increasingly clear is that anxiety is more than a fear of physical death, injury, or other concrete examples of the unknown. It is fear of the unknown itself. It is the complete and radical disconnection from anything solid and familiar on this earth, and it is the cracking open of the complete free fall that is existence. We are terrified of existence because existence is filled with things that are unfamiliar, unhomelike, and uncontained. We are terrified of existence because it is *different* from us—the most different that we can imagine. I know many mystics and philosophers have said precisely the opposite of this assertion. Many have talked of the illusion that existence is different, unfamiliar, and threatening, but that it is, in fact, very compatible with us, comprised of our basic elements and therefore in seamless unity with us if we could but open to this unity. And these visionaries may be right. There may be people who have developed such finely attuned awareness and synchrony with the all that they truly don't experience any separation between self and not-self, and therefore anxiety itself.

But these visionaries and the exemplars they cite are not, in my view, very convincing. Why? Because it would seem the height of hubris to claim that an experience of oneness with everything is in fact the state of oneness with everything. Just as the scientific position on "universal laws" or the "Big Bang" cannot possibly presume that such laws and origin stories hold for all universes and all origins beyond our human instruments to measure or even speculate on them (Greene, 2021). In short, we have a worm's eye view of a god-like vista, and that is both the tragedy and beauty of the human lot. The tragedy is that we are limited and become overwhelmed at points; but the beauty is that we are energized by these limits, and they prod us to evolve. Yet it's hard to evolve without anxiety, and without an encounter with difference and the foreign.

Accordingly, let us begin this journey into life-enhancing anxiety by first exploring anxiety: how it arises, the ways it shocks us, and, yes, the ways it unfolds new possibilities and new life for us—but not without a struggle.

Birth: The Terror–Wonder Template

After a lifetime of inquiry into the intricacies of anxiety, I have arrived at one overarching conclusion. The psychoanalyst and existential philosopher Otto Rank (1924) has come closer to apprehending the root of anxiety than any other theorist of which I'm aware, and here is basically what he says: To probe anxiety we must begin at the beginning—and Rank means the primal beginning—birth. This is the point at which, again, each of us encounters "difference," the unfamiliar, and radical otherness for the first time (separation anxiety and stranger anxiety seem related to this primal moment of severance). It is the point at which we confront mortal danger from these differences—but also the unbound and the uncontrolled (Mikulincer & Shaver, 2012; Solomon et al., 2015). We shift from the relative state of nonexistence and unity to sudden explosive existence and disunity, from a state of quiescence and containment to mayhem and the uncontained.

Although it is admittedly difficult to study (and recall) the experience of birth, it is not a far stretch to imagine what a shock this was for us, what jarring and drama. If there is any doubt about the foundation-shaking quality of emergence into life, consider that there have actually been physiological studies of this state, and the findings are jaw-dropping. For example, research conducted at the distinguished Karolinska Institute in Sweden by Hugo Lagercrantz (2016, p. 58) shows that the stress hormones (catecholamines) of newborns are many times higher than those of normally and even severely stressed adults. This finding suggests that there is something wildly distinctive occurring at the point of birth and in the anatomy of newborns that we can't quite grasp yet. Moreover, it is also quite plausible that this impressive activity is traceable not just to physiology (e.g., being squashed and jostled in the vaginal canal), but also to psychology, and the mayhem experienced upon contact with the outside world.

This at least is what psychological researchers have proposed, from the pioneering studies of Rank to the succeeding research of contemporaries such as Rollo May (1950), Ernest Becker (1973), R.D. Laing (1969), and Stanislav and Christina Grof (1989). As Rank and his great expositor, Becker, suggested, the ordeal is much more than a medical trauma: it is a trauma of the encounter with the measureless and borderless cosmos itself. It also lends insight into the ways people experience trauma (as well as its transformation) later in life. As many of them intimate, the experience of trauma is too big to put into words or categories. But it can be alluded to with metaphors. For example, many of my therapy clients have compared their traumas to a "free fall," a "black hole," and a "bottomless pit from which there is no escape." It is like being cut from the mothership, leaving one lost, adrift, rudderless.

Erich Fromm (1964) equates such anxiety with the biblical allegory of Adam and Eve. The same basic forces are at work. The premier couple moves from a state of innocence and unity, pleasure and tranquility to sudden, abrupt autonomy or, in the Christian tradition, "sin." But the sin of disobeying God's command by eating the forbidden apple is at a deeper level, a step toward liberation, according to Fromm. It is a step toward facing and struggling with the unknown—unknown objects, people, and possibilities. It is a struggle with difference, both between oneself and others and within oneself. And, finally, it is the awakening of consciousness—choice as much as difficulty and pain— and hence the evolution of our humanity. On the other hand, remaining stuck in the garden, tethered to commands and forces outside of oneself, is a form of death, according to Fromm. In Rank's lexicon it's a fear of life, of separating from the womb, and of struggling with one's own identity.

No matter how you look at it, however, anxiety looms over the process of both living and dying. With the former, one struggles with the anxiety, the groundlessness, of being alone and untethered; with the latter, one contends with being swallowed up and eradicated.

The trauma and drama of birth, then is too much for anyone to fully take in, just as infinity is. But the critical issue is *how it is negotiated by our parents, culture, and systems within which we live.* This negotiation is huge, for it will establish whether much of one's life is fear driven and polarized—that is, fixated on single points of view to the utter exclusion of competing points of view—or whether it is secure enough to coexist with, inquire into, and creatively respond to the cosmic flicker called life.

Unfortunately, too many people in our society, and world, don't negotiate this cosmic dilemma very well. I think this is partly because birth drama reminds us of our smallness and helplessness in the world. And who, particularly in dominator societies, wants to acknowledge feeling small and helpless? Hence, very quickly that state of vulnerability gets covered over with rules and regulations that are necessary in many instances, but in other instances suppress a child's natural capacity for exploration. That which is "other" or "different" is particularly problematic because it becomes increasingly linked with avoidance, and that avoidance becomes entrenched if left unaddressed.

If a child is constantly kept from witnessing things and people that are foreign to its immediate family or cultural system, then those things and people tend to become welded to the primal threats a child experiences at birth. In other words, they remain unintegrated "others," just as the "others" in their shock of being expelled from the womb. Furthermore, if one of those others happens to actually become threatening in the child's life—for example, via hearsay or an unfortunate encounter— then that other becomes doubly threatening.

Here we can see how the absence of conversation and inquiry into otherness can be so damaging from a very early age. But we can also see how this problem of otherness is not just an intellectual or behavioral issue but one that is rooted in the deepest recesses of one's emotions, body, and imagination. Furthermore, we can see that precisely for the above reasons intellectualized or behavioral interventions (such as cognitive–behavioral therapy) often pale before these deeply held reactivities, and that *experiential* encounters—that is, felt and embodied encounters with split-off parts of oneself—are for many imperative to allow fundamental healing to occur.

But let us pause for a moment and look at the astounding range of ways that jarring, scrambling plunges into life may impact us. First, they may well form the template for virtually every trauma (shock, anxiety) we experience later in life (that which Rank [1936, p. 189] calls "Urangst"). When a child is cold or uncomfortable, for example, there are echoes of the birthing "free fall." When a father or mother fails to mirror their child, fails to make them feel seen or understood, there are resonances to the helplessness, lostness, and oblivion of being ejected from the womb (we will discuss momentarily the provocative research on this problem in the form of what has come to be known as the "still face experiment"). When a friend gets angry at us, we can feel as if the floor has been taken out from under us. When we slip and fall at school or in a playground, we can feel hints of primal disarray, of flailing. When we feel mocked or dehumanized for such mishaps, we can go again into that menacing "hole." When we fail a course or get reprimanded by a teacher, hints of being tossed and lacking stability are all about us. These hints and sometimes alarms are palpable: when we make mistakes or perform awkwardly; when we disappoint our parents or someone we revere; when we spill food on our pants (like I did on a 5th grade field trip!); when we say something someone doesn't like; when we fall ill, and our whole bodies feel shaken and uninhabitable; and, on a larger scale, when one gang, party, or nation feels disrespected by another, and the affected group goes to these very same places of diminishment, lostness, and insignificance. Just consider how thrown many of us feel today every time we hear about the next mass shooting, or hate crime, or terrorist attack. Attacks on our national character, such as the decimation of the Twin Towers in New York City on 9/11/2001 or the insurrection at our nation's Capital on January 6, 2021 have the added significance of symbolic as well as actual physical derangement.

There is much empirical evidence to support the notion that very early in life, we experience intense anxiety when we fail to feel *met* by our caretakers; when our caretakers physically and emotionally disconnect from us; and when we encounter strangers. Consider, for example, the studies on separation anxiety, stranger anxiety, and the anxiety infants experience when their caretaker expresses a "still face" as opposed to an animated, responsive face (e.g., Tronick, 1989; Nagy et al., 1978). It's as if the babies fall off an emotional cliff when the caretaker ceases to mirror and respond to them. In a very real sense, these babies appear to feel "dropped" and left to flounder. These studies, moreover, which have addressed children from two hours to five years old, provide a powerful indication that the shock babies experience upon expulsion from the womb is the precursor for the distress and agitation children experience later in life. The precursors may be more primitive because of less developed abilities to recognize caretakers and various objects in the environment but they are nevertheless tangible forerunners of these later states.

The research on secure and insecure attachments also supports this shock neonates experience following separation from their mothers. On the other hand, I am arguing for an even deeper cleavage than that between the relative security of the womb and independent life; and that is the cleavage between the relative security of our relation to *existence* and our sudden, abrupt emergence into life. It's not that attachment theory is inaccurate—quite the contrary so far as it goes. But it is the greater problem of our attachment/detachment from the mystery of existence that jars us all so, and that forms the backdrop for so many of our subsequent anxieties. Laing calls this the problem of ontological security/insecurity—our embeddedness and severance from being itself, which again explains the symbolism, such as "free fall," that so many of us use to describe our deepest woes. See also the work of Ernest Schachtel (1959) on children's tendencies to cling to safe and secure environments, particularly when conditioned to fear the world, as distinct from their counter-tendencies to explore, experiment, and "play" with the possibilities of novel environments. He called the former tendency (cosmically appropriate enough) the "embeddedness affect" and the latter tendency the "activity affect."

Correspondingly, we need to highlight the power of what Winnicott (1965) calls the "holding environment" as a balm for this tear in the fabric of our existential embeddedness. As we have intimated above, the holding environment or atmosphere that is (co)created by parent and child—and subsequently culture and child—is all important in regard to how that child develops. Moreover, it is precisely this holding environment and presence that forms our earliest internalization of whether and to what extent the radically new world we emerge into is safe, trustworthy, negotiable, navigable, and expandable. In short, the holding environment becomes the "sea" within which we may either flounder and rigidify or gradually and intensively begin to grow and flourish.

The perceptive psychoanalyst Heinz Kohut (1977) observed this "sea" at play in his psychotherapeutic practice. That which Kohut called the "transmuting internalization" is the point at which patients begin to experience the therapeutic sea as a supportive, resilient medium; one in which therapeutic ruptures ("stormy seas" of conflict between analyst and patient) can still be worked out and transformed despite the most profound anxieties. The transmuting or transforming of such anxieties, which echo the primal anxieties of birth, can then be reframed within patients themselves. The new and more adaptive message is that "if I can clash that much with someone else—that is, my analyst—and yet still feel loved by them, perhaps I can clash with the unstable places in myself and still feel love."

The Existential Unconscious

Collectively, these echoes of primal helplessness can now be described in terms of a fresh conception of the unconscious—the *existential unconscious.* While the existential unconscious has been invoked by a number of depth psychological theorists,[2] Rank scholar Robert Kramer (in press) views the existential unconscious as a recasting of the psychoanalytic conception of the unconscious in existential terms. Whereas the psychoanalytic conception of the unconscious is classically

---

[2] Compare, for example, the existential unconscious with the "ontological unconscious" put forth by Robert Stolorow (2007). In my understanding these conceptions share similarities but also notable differences, such as Stolorow's emphasis on language as a hallmark of the ontological unconscious, whereas the existential unconscious may be seen as fundamentally pre-linguistic and embodied.

associated with instinctual drives and, more recently, with failures in early parenting, what we now call the existential unconscious is linked with something considerably more radical and probably universal: the primordial shift from nonexistence to sudden, bewildering existence.

Distinguishing between the Freudian and Rankian understanding of the unconscious, Kramer (in press, pp. 6–7) writes:

> A biologist of the mind, Freud had always insisted that the difference between male and female was "biological bedrock." Although not disputing the force of biology or the sex difference, Rank, in his *Trauma of Birth*, peered below biological bedrock to confront the ontological, or better the preontological, mystery of Being itself: that is, the awesome difference—the ineffable difference—between nonexistence and existence. Rank (1996) had discovered the "'existential' unconscious" (p. 225), an unconscious far more anxiety-provoking than the Freudian unconscious in which simmered male sexual desire, castration fear, and guilt. "The mere fact of difference," according to Rank (1936), "in other words, the existence of our own will as opposite, unlike, is the basis for the [self-] condemnation which manifests itself as inferiority or guilt-feeling" (p. 79).
>
> Rank never minimized the enormous significance of the anatomical difference between the sexes. This difference, however, is the second most important difference the child confronts.
>
> "First comes the perception of difference from others as a consequence of becoming conscious of self . . . then interpretation of this difference as inferiority . . . finally association of this psychological conflict with the biological sexual problem, the difference of the sexes" (p. 78). The difference between nonexistence and existence precedes and colors all other difference—whether it be the difference of sex, age, race, intelligence, religion, or nationality.

The existential unconscious, then, unchains us from many classical conceptions of nonconscious processing, from the delimited investigations of the laboratory to the restrictive datasets, resonant as they may be in certain instances, of theorists such as Freud and Jung. Indeed, the existential unconscious opens us to a rich phenomenological field that extends beyond the categorizations and biases of individuals to the farther reaches of humanity as a whole. In so doing, it brings us to the borders of our anxieties; but those anxieties offer us an extremely fertile ground for exploration, discovery, and continual personal and collective evolution.

The existential unconscious, moreover, opens us to a rich repository of thinking about life. No longer need we be confined to the boundary lines of our parenting, heritage, or biology, but without denying these we can also open up to what Rank called our creative will. By finding the courage to face our existential unconscious—the unsettlements of our separation from the vast unknown—we can find possibilities in that vast unknown. We can engage our will to explore inner and outer terrain that our parents, cultures, and even scientific authorities may not have dreamed about, but that now can and must be pursued, if we are to sustain our planet and species. Among these terrains are inventive alternatives to climate change, the healing of prejudice and bigotry, and the enrichment of our personal and collective lives.

The chapters that follow display different sides of our encounter with the existential unconscious and, thus, the anxiety it arouses. These chapters share one overarching theme: the recognition that grappling with the latter can bring renewed appreciation for life that can have very far-reaching benefits, from the individual's sense of fulfillment to the moral and ethical soundness of societies.

Chapter 2

The Tyranny of Sameness

We strive for sameness not only because it is familiar to us, but also because it makes us feel comfortable—safe, warm, held; like the feelings we get returning to our same homes, seeing our same loved ones, sitting in our same chairs, eating our same meals, engaging in our same conversations, reading our same newspapers, fingering our same devices, driving in our same cars, visiting our same friends, playing our same songs. And here's where it gets especially thorny: when we *insist* on our same tribes, clubs, classes, races, religions, political parties, specialties, habits, obsessions, routines, rituals, prejudices, hatreds, fanaticisms, nationalisms, sexisms, genderisms, idealisms, universalisms, and absolutisms.

As the early Gestalt psychologists proposed, human beings have an inclination for closure, for "completing" things, and that means the striving for and maintenance of sameness. For example, from a young age, we develop fantasy systems, as the psychologist Robert Firestone (2022) called them, that may be unsettling, even terrifying. Because they are absolutized, closed, barred from other possibilities, they protect us from an even worse perspective (e.g., "mommy and daddy are dangerous with others but they would never hurt me"—or not intentionally at least). Such fantasies may be carried into adult life where we expect, say, that our socially hostile romantic partner would never lay a hand on us. But then one day they do, and yet because of our entrenched fantasy system, we still may deny it, or deny that it was intentional! Hence, we hold on to the same fantasy, the same view, because to divert from it would mean the unthinkable—for example, that our parent or partner would actually want to injure us at times and that the world is a more complicated place than we at first believed. How far is it from this kind of thinking when we defend leaders or groups we know at some level are not acting in our interest but whose delegitimization is so threatening to our need for sameness, for the routine and familiar, that we simply give in to them.

Finally, we will strive at all costs to protect our sameness, our "safe" and reliable patterns, even if *we* become the destroyers. This becomes atrociously clear when we will actually kill for our sameness striving. Again, take our example of the above fantasy system and expand it to a culture or tribe. Let's say that we develop the fantasy that our cultural leader, who may be savage toward "foreigners," would never act likewise toward us. Due to our insistence on sameness, we may not only support that belief in the face of evidence to the contrary, we may even try to destroy the people who challenge it. This action is reflective of the extent to which our identities are not only tied to the rescue fantasy surrounding our leader (parent) but to the primal helplessness we're likely to experience in the *absence* of that leader. Put another way, some will do anything they can—including annihilate others—to deny the helplessness and groundlessness associated with departures from their sameness fantasies, especially when those fantasies are acute (Becker, 1975; Haidt, 2013).

Hence, the desire for sameness can actually be one of the most destructive aspects of being alive. It is at the base of most wars, physical and emotional abuse, addictions, prejudices and bigotry, hegemony and imperialism, narcissism, crime, dehumanization, and so on. Too often sameness is about control and the imposition of familiarity even where people or things pose no tangible threat. For example, we meet people who think or act differently from us, who go about their own business, and yet we insist they be like us. We encounter religions and ideas that are completely new to us, yet we twist those domains into "like us" or "against us." What happened at the U.S. Capitol on January 6, 2021 was a vivid example of sameness mania. Some people couldn't feel comfortable or just okay with finding peaceful means to work out political differences, and so they exploded in revolt. The advent of "cancel culture" on college campuses and institutions throughout the United States recently is also an example of this sameness tendency. The (sometimes violent) reaction of those on the political Left—as well as Right—against opinions that differ from their deeply held convictions has led to disturbing forms of censorship and even "shunning" in certain quarters. This is the problem with the vicious cycle of polarized minds. Once the cycle has been initiated, an equal and sometimes more intense backlash ensues, and so the cycle proceeds.

Again, we may understand in varying degrees the reasons for both "conservative" and "liberal" scenarios, but they still played out based on similar primal grounds—the desperate need to *conflate* particular incidents, egregious acts with entire groups, entire races, classes, political parties. Hitler did this in his conflation of evil with Jews, Stalin and Mao with their conflation of intellectuals and aristocrats with social bankruptcy—and they all used these forms of conflation as pretexts for tyranny.

Conflation is one of the chief bases for destructiveness. It makes us feel comfortable, unified, welded to ultimate powers. It makes us feel totally right, totally knowing and totally embraced, but also vehemently cynical, particularly toward those who differ from us. On a subtler level, I fear that this problem is evolving with our ballooning reliance on technology. The more we look to devices to perform tasks that we may have otherwise performed—such as engaging in face-to-face meetings, struggling with truth, searching beyond simple messages, cultivating a time-honored craft, or learning to be creative—the harder it is to step out of those routinized patterns and enter into fresh and renewing patterns. Correspondingly, the more we deviate from our automated lifestyles, the more errant, alien, and wild tech-free encounters tend to appear.

When we delude ourselves that we have total truth, we also delude ourselves that we have total familiarity. Again, this is an understandable reaction to a perceived personal or collective threat. It is a primal reaction that appears to have roots in our shift from a unitive to a severed state—from the womb to the hospital room, and at a deeper level from the cosmic canopy to sudden, abrupt life. It is, therefore, a common reaction, but it is also lame reaction, a reaction without discernment. And we need to discern lest we lapse into same-obsessed adversaries rarely enabling difference.

The engagement with difference, on the other hand, requires courage and, even more fundamentally, love. It takes love in some form to not only tolerate but also appreciate the chasms of difference. One has to cross the gap of unknowing, the temporary helplessness of being in suspense and without foundation. This is a gap that many bridge for their loved ones, particularly from the start of life; but, tragically, it is also a gap that many others do not. Like the blank-staring parents in the "still face" experiments, they leave their children or partners or fellow citizens to flounder in helplessness and self-doubt, or in worst cases self-hate. They abandon them to the abyss of isolation with few or no tools to work themselves out of the quagmire, the free fall of untethered existence. The result is a child, or in some cases adult, who is not able to tolerate, let alone revel in, differences; a child or adult who becomes bound to routine, to fear-based thinking, feeling, and acting; a child or adult who associates differences with something alien or threatening or self-annihilating. For after all, when they expressed liveliness, passion, or their uniqueness it was met with indifference, derision. So why would anyone be willing to step into such embattlement. It is much easier to become passive, to follow the routines and well-trodden paths; or to explode, on the other hand, into a counter-dependent rebellion against those paths, which is still a form of conformity and sameness rather than create one's own paths based on one's own hard-won discernment.

Again, the question is: Can we move toward courage and love rather than fear and compulsiveness as the basis for our decisions? Can we move toward the paradox that we are separate but related and acquire the skills necessary to reckon with that reality?

All that said, I do want to acknowledge that there are times when differences are not safe, and there is need for group cohesion. When an individual or group's survival is in peril, that may not be the best time to pursue openness to differences. In addition, we all need the comfort of homogeneity at times, the comradery of our household, our friends, and our communities. The issue hinges on the extent to which one is wedded to such sameness or conditioned by forces that may or may not be in the individual or group's interest. Here, as in so many aspects of human experience, being able to take a meta-view—that is, to be aware of what one is aware of—can be of enormous benefit. It represents the difference between compulsive action and that which is guided by a modicum of choice.

Chapter 3

The Age of Reason Must Give Way to the Age of Depth: Why Our World is in Crisis[1]

We humans need to get our act together concerning anxiety. Our attempts to block anxiety, pretend it doesn't exist, or propel ourselves in the opposite direction have been a disaster, and we're continuing to perpetuate that disaster now. Just think about how many problems anxiety denial has brought us: tyrannical leaders, imperious states, remorseless bigots, hateful ideologues, merciless financial moguls, soulless intellects, reckless industrialists, robotic bureaucrats, heartless abusers, and mindless addicts. In fact, all who have pursued the quick-fix, instant-results approach to living bear this legacy and, of course, that includes every one of us at one time or another. Think, for example, how many of us have been attracted to the simplistic and expedient—whether through petty squabbles, crass commercialism, fast food, speedy internet, smart TVs, ingenious phones, pills, apps, sports channels, slogans, fashions, hero worship, or guns. But it is strikingly a matter of degree, is it not?

It is more than a truism that anxiety and vulnerability go together and that we humans have had a hard time with that—especially the vulnerability part. Hasn't this problem shown itself early on? When we needed to scare off death and illness, we wore amulets. When we felt guilty, we offered sacrifices to wipe the feeling away. When we were bombarded by storms, we created weather gods to keep them at bay.

But let us pause for a moment. Today we've got a glaring problem in our country and world. It's not our only problem and it isn't the cause of all our sorrows, but currently it is one of the chief problems we face—and it is scarcely scrutinized by psychologists. The problem to which I refer is our socio-economic model for living.

---

[1] Author's Note: This chapter is slightly adapted from a blog in *Psychology Today Online*. Copyright Sussex Publishers, LLC

Today's hate incidents, climate change, and budding authoritarianism may seem like distinct issues. Yet think again. In his signature work, *Madness and Civilization*, Michel Foucault (1973) proposed that ever since the Renaissance, the Western world has been hell-bent on quantifying and commodifying life. This furor has not only anguished the souls of those who sought to advance it but also, and equally, those who sought to oppose it.

"The age of reason confined" (p. 65), declared Foucault; and for all its virtues, and there are many, it must be conceded that it still confines today. Equating the age of reason with the onset of the industrial revolution and its industrialized needs, Foucault found a metaphor for all that reason feared and attempted to segregate from "normal" life—the metaphor of "madness." Yet by this term he did not merely mean the poor, the dirty, and the deranged, but much that was (and is) sensuous, spontaneous, intimate, poignant, and ironic. In short, madness stood for all that defied mechanized thinking and mechanized labor. Foucault summarizes:

> A sensibility was born which had drawn a line and laid a cornerstone, and which chose—only to banish. The concrete space of classical society reserved a neutral region, a blank page where the real life of the city was suspended; here, order no longer confronted disorder, reason no longer tried to make its own way among all that might evade or seek to deny it. Here reason reigned in the pure state, in a triumph arranged for it in advance over a frenzied unreason. Madness was thus torn from that imaginary freedom which still allowed it to flourish on the Renaissance horizon. Not so long ago, it had floundered about in broad daylight: in King Lear, in Don Quixote. But in less than a half century, it had been sequestered and, in the fortress of confinement, bound to Reason, to the rules of morality and to their monotonous nights. (p. 64)

Is it any wonder, then, that in our "advanced" age of reason, there are so many costs to be borne? Along with the marvels of technology, efficiency, and sanitization has come the relinquishment of so much that enriched our primal past (and present) and that is now responsible for our "monotonous nights" (and days!). And is it any wonder that part of the price we pay for such fanaticism of the rational (mechanical) is fanatical backlashes against the vacuity it leaves in its wake? This is certainly the message of what many of the killers and fanatics evince upon investigation (e.g., see the work of Ari Kruglanski et al. [2012] in the volume *Meaning, Mortality, and Choice: The Social Psychology of Existential Concerns*). It could be said that the perceived hollowness of contemporary life in the United States is a pretext for backlashes all over the world, including in our own country—backlashes that are too often egregious: from senseless shootings to the propagation of authoritarian regimes, and from obsession with nationalism to religious preoccupation with purity, order, and conformity.

Our problem, as Foucault so prophetically contended, is not that we have restored comparative stability to a plague-infested bestial world; this was, of course, welcome in many quarters. Our problem is that in our panic to avoid the banes of the past, we threw out their blessings and brought about our own bestial and polarizing way of life. This way of life is crushing the spirit of its constituents and rousing the animosities of its opponents (see the news about U.S. depression rates and mass shootings, fundamentalist violence in the Middle East, and nationalist tyranny in Eastern Europe). Isn't it clear that Rationalism has its limits, is no longer supplying meaning to drone-like lives, and has not solved our absurd problem with treating people and life with care?

The point is that Rationalism does not account for wide ranges of human experience that cannot be mathematically measured or detected by our five senses. The imagination, emotions, intuitions, and complex contexts such as personal dispositions, family and cultural backgrounds, racial and political considerations, and our sense of connection to others and the cosmos itself all figure in actions and nonactions. If we want to know substantively what people fear and wish for, we need to sit with them, get to know them, and draw on all our modes of detection, both rational and nonrational.

In short, the crisis of Rationalism is undeniable, and the need for depth—a multi-layered understanding of the human condition—and awe-based reform is equally apparent. Will we step up to the challenge? Will our remedies encompass the essential domains for a maximally flourishing society: childrearing, education, work, religious and spiritual settings, and governments? It is this inflection point, this fork in the road of our contending life-philosophies, that will determine the viability of the human species.

Chapter 4

A Meditation on *My* Anxiety

I've known anxiety. Intensely.

Barely 22 years old, I was living in a lonely apartment in rural Georgia. I had just started a master's program in psychology and was hundreds of miles from home. I missed my girlfriend, my family, and my old familiar hangouts. Then just as I was becoming acquainted with this enchanted yet remote place, my father and his 23-year-old fiancée arrived for a visit. It was late fall and the darkness was palpable. On top of these developments, I had just been encouraged by a professor I revered to work at a local mental hospital (as they called it in those days), and though I was energized by the gesture I was also frankly petrified. Much of my ambivalence was clearly traceable to the reactivation of an early trauma that shook me to the core. That trauma involved my seven-year-old brother, who died when I was two and a half. Though I had vital support in the wake of that catastrophe, including a sustained period of psychoanalysis when I was about six, the emotional mayhem of that time still haunted me. This was particularly evident at critical points such as being far from home and feeling estranged, lost, and child-like. I was in a state of acute vulnerability, in other words, and the challenge to work with people whom I perceived to be even more vulnerable and lost—namely, psychotic—reawakened very primal fears in me (see Chapter 5 for more details on my rocky early years).

After a warm reunion with my father and his fiancée, we decided to go to a movie that night called *Magic*. The movie starred Anthony Hopkins, who played a disturbed ventriloquist who manipulated an equally menacing puppet named "Fats." Somehow the macabre nature of Hopkins' character and the demonic presence of the puppet converged like a laser that penetrated my defenses and shook me to my core. Whereas my sense of who I thought I was had held up well for many years following my childhood analysis, suddenly that was all unraveling, and neither my father nor the deep bond we shared could stem it.

Yet as anguished as I had become that evening, there was one more episode that took me over the top so to speak. When we all left the movie theater and walked into the dimly lit parking lot, I immediately spotted a note that was left on my car. I can't recall the exact wording, but it was one of the most cryptic messages I'd ever seen, stating in effect "you will die tonight."

Following that jarring series of events, I still had no idea what I was in for that night when I went to sleep. Suddenly after a few minutes of lying on my bed, it was like a gate flung open and a shaft of terror came crashing through my mind. It was as if all the trepidations and monstrosities that I experienced as a child hurtled out of the darkness and pierced right through me. Rarely had I felt so powerless as image after horrifying image poured into me. I felt like I was in a tornado of dread shattering every solid anchor of who I thought I was and carrying me into oblivion. Wave after wave of panic seized my whole being, and by the time I awoke in the morning I was a wreck. I was afraid to move lest I'd be overcome by my own mind. I shook incessantly, and I feared for the first time since very early childhood that I was genuinely on the brink of complete breakdown.

My father and his girlfriend came over and tried to calm me but to no avail. Finally, I thought of the one person whom I felt might be able to understand and be of support, and that person turned out to be one of the critical contacts in my life. Her name was Debbie H. She was a fellow student, and she was blind. Yet like the blind seer Tiresias in the Oedipal story, she had an almost sage-like presence. After promptly and receptively answering my call, Debbie sat with me in focused yet profound silence as I shared my ordeal. Then in a firm yet loving voice she stated, "This too shall pass," and for me those words were like gold. They and she—her extraordinary presence—gave me hope; and this hope, fragile as it was, was the start of my healing. Then Debbie uttered another equally critical suggestion. She recommended that I see a therapist she knew named Ann. That was the start of the most important journey into my depths—the heart of my inner life—that I ever experienced, and quite possibly will ever experience. For Ann could really "meet" me, "get" me, and enable me to get myself in a way I never had before. She was a treasure.

But before I met Ann, I recall some terrifying moments. For many days and weeks, I was beset by panic and anxiety. It seemed as if the slightest association to feeling helpless or being far from home and my girlfriend, or thinking I might be psychotic would set off a racing heart, physical shaking, and relentless feelings of doom. I also experienced perceptual distortions. For example, I would watch one of my professors speak but only hear every individual word he was saying, not the gist or basic idea he was conveying. This started to happen with other professors and even students, which gave me a growing sense of unraveling that just added to my anguish.

Thus was my initiation into the throes of panic and anxiety. I could easily have been diagnosed with an "anxiety disorder" accompanied by features of panic and distorted perceptions, but such a diagnosis would hardly illuminate what I was grappling with. This was a coming-of-age battle and a deep gnawing reactivation of "unfinished business" stemming from childhood fears. My therapist–analyst, Ann G., recognized the complexity of my malady. She conveyed a sense of confidence that I was going through a kind of "dark night of the soul," and that there was more, so much more, that I could discover from this time. Just this perspective alone was helpful to me. Ann conveyed it with her smiles and wry humor. She occasionally disclosed some of her own foibles, and even a break up of a recent relationship. The disclosure was obviously painful to her, but she held it in a light and playful space.

Ann was a large woman, not obese but solid, with an embracing presence. She looked like she could take just about anything and just be with it, maintain a stance of curiosity about it. And indeed, she could. But Ann was not just a pin cushion or imposing mama bear; she took me and my difficulties seriously. She involved herself with me, tracking the most minute nuances and shifts that would come up in the course of our meeting. She conveyed that she was there for me, and open to whatever bothered me in a given moment, including sometimes our relationship.

In later visits with Ann, I attained many insights about my family life, such as my mother's profound grief and her loving yet confusing style of communicating with me. Although this style was understandable in the wake of my mother having lost her firstborn and now needing to turn her full attention to her second born—me—it was also quite debilitating (see Chapter 5 for more detail). I also learned much about my own devitalizing thoughts and behaviors. But beyond these important discoveries, I learned something else that has bolstered me for over 40 years: how to be bodily present, even in the most dire moments of vulnerability.

With this hard-won discovery, I have been able to pursue romantic relationships that I hardly knew were possible at the time of my breakdown. Foremost among these was what turned out to be a 40-year relationship with my wife, Jurate. Jurate derived from a completely different geographic background than I—Los Angeles, California. She was also a Catholic and a first-generation Lithuanian American. I must acknowledge my great fortune in meeting and forming lasting bonds with this remarkable woman, whom I met at a little medical library at the University of California, San Francisco! But I also must give credit to my life-transforming therapy with Ann, which enabled me to appreciate and be much less daunted by "difference." This led to such an enduring and enriching life with a person that "on paper," as my wife is fond of saying, makes little sense; and yet makes a world of sense to both of us, and I believe to our son, Benjamin.

The discovery of presence also freed me to pursue academic and professional attainments, such as my doctoral degree, becoming a psychotherapist, teaching, and eventually lecturing internationally, that I could hardly fathom as a distressed 22-year-old. In fact, I was terrified of all such prospects at that age, although also strongly allured by them. It would have been an all too familiar tragedy, at least from my vantage point of looking back, if I had remained a captive of my terror and lived a thin and reticent existence as a result. That said, the last thing I want to do here is sound prideful and self-congratulatory. I did have many social, educational, and financial advantages along my path, and these were fortifying to be sure. Yet I strongly believe there is a lesson here for everyone who struggles with the meaning and direction of their lives: *How are they willing to live those lives, and what degree of anxiety will they accept to break out of the bankrupt barriers that they and others have set for themselves?*

The struggle with anxiety is imperative for many and should not be trifled with. The daunting passageways of what the psychoanalytic historian Robert Kramer calls the "existential unconscious" must be grappled with, at least by many, for substantive change to occur. But, in my experience, if that change is essentially biological or intellectual or behavioral, it is not as likely to endure. On the other hand, if the change is holistic, involving one's whole bodily being, it is likely to be life-altering and profoundly ingrained. Perhaps the greatest lesson I learned through my work with Ann was that presence, or the art of "staying with" my panic and terror, can lead to inner freedom. And inner freedom cannot be over-estimated. It is emphatically among the most valuable and enduring gifts one can possess.

Chapter 5

From Anxiety to Awe:
A Personal Account[1]

Over the past 66 years, I've had the privilege to witness many poignant transformations. As a practicing psychologist I've witnessed them in state hospitals, in psychiatric emergency clinics, in drug and alcohol agencies, and in private practice; and as a youth I experienced them in my own intensive psychotherapies. There is little "pretty" about these ordeals, but when they succeed they are profoundly gratifying and life-changing.

Poignant transformations emerge from the depths of despair, but they result, if one is fortunate, in the heights of renewal. Certainly this was true for me and many of the people I've known or worked with. What could be more precious than the gift of liberation from crippling despair, of being freed to pursue what deeply matters? What could be more critical than participating in, really grappling with, the rescue of one's soul?

Yet what I'm seeing today throughout our culture is an increasing tendency to skip over this grappling part of the equation and to shift abruptly to the transformational part. Not that there's anything untoward about desiring to be rapidly transformed; it's perfectly natural. When one is in distress, one seeks an instant remedy. I do that, my friends do that, and it's a good bet that you do that also; it's instinct. However, there are solid reasons to question instinct at times. For example, most people don't punch someone just because they feel slighted. Similarly, most people don't just blurt out whatever they feel just because they feel it. On the contrary, there is much to consider—from the people you may hurt, to your conscience, to the setting and circumstances of the event. I've seen many clients who initially want to assault someone who assaulted them; however, they rarely do. This is

---

[1] Author's Note: This essay with slight modifications was originally published in *Aeon* under the title "The Awe of Being Alive."

because through the course of therapy, these clients recognize that their assailant is often someone they can relate to—or perhaps even love—and they do not, in the end, want their fellow human being to suffer as they themselves have suffered. There are many times when delay is much preferred to reacting, especially when it comes to emotions.

Emotions are wonderful signals. They alert us to danger and they mobilize us when action is called for. But they are also highly complex, variegated. For example, many people feel contemptible or unwanted at times, yet they don't resort to suicide or drugs. They see that despite their dark mood they have a right to live and grow, just as others live and grow, and that they can become something more than the stereotyped messages about themselves, such as that of being a failure. These are messages, by the way, that too often came from others who themselves felt contemptible and unwanted and who projected those devaluations onto their unwitting victims. But such realizations, particularly if they are to endure, often take time; they take struggle, and they take encounters with larger parts of ourselves that go beyond our internalized oppression to a kind of conciliation. In the end, depth and existential therapy promote a hard-won coexistence between rivaling parts of ourselves, parts that sometimes agonize yet in the long run shed light on the experience of being fully human, of being deeply and richly alive. Put more formally, existential therapy emphasizes three major themes: *freedom* to explore what deeply matters to oneself, *experiential* or whole-bodied reflection on what deeply matters, and *responsibility* or the ability to respond to, act on, and apply what deeply matters.

Yet today it is all too easy to bypass the effort to attain such freedom, experiential reflection, and response ability—such grappling with who we are and who we are willing to be. Today we are seduced by an avalanche of devices, formulations, and machine-meditated transactions making it all too tempting to let others, including mechanical others, do the job. Whether it is psychiatric medication, psychotherapy apps, twelve-session clinic appointments, or the distraction of net surfing, there are innumerable ways to surmise that our pain has been dissolved, that we have been transformed, and that life proceeds apace.

But the looming and overarching question is: At what cost? At what cost is an externally or even cerebrally normalized life, a life of routine and regulation, elevated over a life that flops and flutters but also throbs? At what price is a life that sails over the many-sided intricacies of emotion and the ripples of discontent? Too often the price is death, both literal and figurative, and the statistics bear that out. Consider rising rates of depression and addiction and the sense of isolation often linked to smartphones.

My earliest memory is a gauzy image of my parents weeping on the living room couch. That was when I was two-and-a-half years old, and my seven-year-old brother Kelly had just passed away. It was 1959 and the combination of chicken pox and pneumonia proved too much for an otherwise radiant and vigorous child. The explosion of this event in the collective psyche of our family cannot be lucidly grasped. The most I can say is that the parents I knew before the event were dimly recognizable in its crushing aftermath. The warm and playful sibling I knew—the smiling leader—was vanquished, and in his place yawned a gaping void, a pit of rage, sorrow, and terror.

By three years old, I was imploding. My defenses were all but expired. I had night terrors and I had tantrums. I was panicked and I was lost— tail spinning into a helpless and paranoid world. Given my ordeal then, I'm fairly certain that if I had the same experience today that I had in 1959, I would be summarily pacified by drugs. Instead, my parents sat with me back then. They did all they could to talk me through my battles, and eventually, at age six, they referred me to a psychoanalyst. (For readers interested in learning more about my engagement with this psychoanalyst—and the stark background for my anxieties, I have decided to disclose an excerpt of my psychoanalyst's observations when he first met me. These observations are contained in an extraordinary letter he provided to me many years following Kelly's death. See Appendix A at the end of this volume for the full display of this record).

Eventually, this psychoanalyst helped turn my life around. Although I continued to have profound fears and outbursts, he helped me to work through, rather than mask over, these potentially restorative maladies. Greatest of all, he was a rock-solid presence who enabled me to say or feel anything. I was hanging on by a thread, but he remained a pillar, steadfast and supportive, until I passed through the storm.

Yet how many children today are encouraged to work through their torment, or even to supplement their medication with an emotionally supportive encounter? How many are granted the time and money to do so? Very few, I would venture. What most are encouraged to do is to ingest antidepressants, anti-anxiety meds, and a variety of mood stabilizers. While these remedies can at times be life-saving, too often they are pushed by pharmaceutical companies and insurers more concerned with profit margins than the enduring care of people, and people's own resources to live the life they seek.

I wonder how I would have turned out if I had been treated by today's standard. I wonder if I would have experienced the rigors of being alone or being challenged, as I was by my analyst, to develop inner resources, such as my creativity, curiosity, and imagination. He encouraged me to reflect on the bases for my fears and to move at my own pace. He respected me and my capacities, which in turn spurred me to create drawings, stories, and thoughts about life's puzzlements. He supported me to venture out into uncertain terrains, relationships, and ideas, which I eventually did after much tussling and even further therapy.

The chief problem with many contemporary interventions is that they're one-dimensional. For example, psychotropic medications aim at making people feel calmer if they're anxious, or more energized if they're depressed. Cognitive therapies aspire to change so-called irrational thoughts (like fear of flying or a sense of worthlessness) into rational—that is, evidence-based—thoughts. Behavioral therapies aim at reinforcing adaptive habits to replace maladaptive habits, and so on. The problem with these strategies, however, is that for many they work on a limited basis. If one wishes to live more efficiently along clear and culturally approved lines, then one may be notably helped by such techniques. If one wishes to live a comparatively regimented and low-risk life, these remedies are likely to be appropriate. However, if one is among the sizable and perhaps growing population that seeks more dimensionality in life—more meaning, more vitality, more personal and interpersonal richness—then something more challenging may be called for.

After a lifetime of research, the existential psychologist Rollo May concluded that many of the most vital and creative people through history were strongest at precisely their most vulnerable points. In *The Psychology of Existence*, a book I co-wrote with May (Schneider & May, 1995), he included a chapter called "The Wounded Healer," about what makes a good therapist. In it May gave the example of the renowned psychologist Abraham Maslow, who was lonely and unhappy as a child but who formulated theories about optimal living and peak experiences. May went on to describe a host of famous and lesser known people who faced and integrated the sides of themselves they feared and, through that process, fostered creative and productive lives.

May's thesis is backed by a host of distinguished investigators, including Carl Jung, Silvano Arieti, Frank Barron, and Maslow himself, who described the "self-actualizing" personality: the optimal personality fulfilling their potential and life's true dreams. "One observation that I made has puzzled me for many years but it begins to fall into place now," Maslow (1968) wrote: "It was what I described as the resolution of dichotomies in self-actualizing people....These most mature of all people were also strongly childlike. These same people, the strongest egos ever described and the most definitely individual, were also precisely the ones who could be the most easily egoless, self-transcending, and problem-centered" (p. 140).

The clinical psychologist and researcher Kay Jamison (1993), author of seminal studies on bipolar disorder and the book, *Touched by Fire: Manic-Depressive Illness and the Artistic Temperament*, agrees. Bipolar herself, Jamison described dozens of artistic luminaries throughout history who appeared to fall on the bipolar spectrum, yet went on to forge exemplary contributions to society.

Granted that many of these luminaries lived very trying lives, and some even committed suicide, but many also lived rich and invigorating lives with deeply gratifying results. Hence, one of the chief questions for our age is what happens if we remove such life struggles, if we flatten the biology, if we remove the rough edges through technology and drugs? What happens if we bypass the need for people to confront their demons, their discomforts, and their tears? Would the artistic creation that results be the emotional equivalent of one that was inspired by the pathos, perplexity, and toil of the human artist?

The most popular treatments today, such as medication and cognitive behavioral therapy or CBT, are often short term and have a mixed record with regard to effectiveness (Shedler, 2012). The emerging view is that they are helpful for relief of symptoms such as negative thoughts, poor appetite, and phobias, but questionable when it comes to complex life issues such as the search for meaning and purpose and the struggle with love.

Other new remedies include the development of virtual reality (VR) for post-traumatic stress syndrome, the use of neurofeedback from fMRI data to guide therapeutic practice, and apps for everything from anxiety to depression to irritable bowel syndrome. The research on these devices is still very much evolving, but I have the creeping feeling that we are entering a brave new age where statistical and mechanical manipulation is replacing personal discovery and risk.

Is the virtual encounter with one's anxiety—or desire, for that matter—the same as the actual encounter? Is an app the same as a human healer (let alone a wounded healer)? Is the experience of one's therapist or device *enacting* an empathic response the same as their *actually empathizing*? Is this *performance* of a relationship, based on manuals and statistics, the same as a personal evolving relationship with all its angst and vulnerabilities, its challenges and surprises?

I doubt it, and mounting studies uphold the value of person-to-person, genuine therapeutic relationships as well. Again, there can be much value to short-term "mechanized" relationships. They can reach people where few human professionals live, they can help the disabled who have difficulty traveling, and they can relate to young people schooled on hand-held devices. But are they the "be-all" and "end-all" that so many in our society are embracing?

It seems to me that we are moving headlong into the engineering quagmire that so many humanistically oriented therapists have feared. This is an approach where the emphasis is on the device or technique or algorithm and not on the patient's inbred capacities for revitalization. It is a model that stresses standards of normalcy, regulation, and calmness that are imposed from without as distinct from within the subjective and interactive energies of persons. Finally, it is a model that can rob many of us of the virtues—not just the anguish—of our many-sidedness.

Here is a list of sensibilities that I probably would have been "spared" had I been drugged and plugged into devices as a child:

- The trial of being alone
- The angst of great sorrow
- The paralysis of great despair
- The shudder of great fear
- The terror of fragility
- The distress of uncertainty
- The bitterness of rage
- The panic of feeling lost

And here is a list of sensibilities that I likely would not have developed had I been "drugged" and '"plugged':

- The creativity of being alone
- The sensitivity of experiencing sorrow
- The mobilization spurred by despair
- The defiance sparked by fear
- The humility generated by fragility
- The possibilities opened by uncertainty

- The strength aroused by rage
- The curiosities prompted by disarray
- The self-exploration, depth therapy, and inquiry inspired by my entire ordeal

These observations remind me of an extraordinary quote from a similarly disposed colleague:

> If someone told me that I could live my life again free of depression provided I was willing to give up the gifts depression has given me—the depth of awareness, the expanded consciousness, the increased sensitivity, the awareness of limitation, the tenderness of love, the meaning of friendship, the appreciation of life, the joy of a passionate heart—I would say, "This is a Faustian bargain! Give me my depressions." Let the darkness descend. But do not take away the gifts that depression, with the help of some unseen hand, has dredged up from the deep ocean of my soul and strewn along the shores of my life. I can endure darkness if I must; but I cannot live without these gifts. I cannot live without my soul. (Elkins, 1998, p. 188)

It seems to me that one overarching property distinguishes human from mechanical existence. It is not consciousness, because artificial intelligence is already showing that mechanical entities can achieve a kind of signal detection that simulates awareness: consider robots that register temperature changes in the environment. It is not reflexive consciousness, which is the ability of consciousness to have some level of awareness of itself, because scientists are already working on machines that can readjust their calculations based on incoming data. And it is not even the capacity to experience emotions, because there are neural chips in development that will someday be able to replicate the biochemical processes that comprise, say, sadness or elation. (In crude form, this is possible today with psychotropic drugs.)

By contrast, the biggest if not insurmountable hurdle for artificial intelligence is a much more complicated problem: It is the experience of life's paradoxes. As with the testimony of my childhood ordeal, it is the experience not of a single image, thought, or emotion but of the sublimely interwoven image, thought, and emotion, each of which can both dovetail and clash with one another.

Such paradoxes include the sliver of fear in a loving relationship, or the hint of sorrow in a moment of glee, or the taste of envy in the most admiring friendships; and it is many more delicately nuanced combinations that lend life its zest, its pathos and intensity, its awe. Consider how each of these so-called negative emotions echo awesome ranges of awareness:

Sadness comprises sorrow and despondency, the profound sense of bereavement and loss. But post-traumatic growth studies also indicate that sadness alerts us to the fleeting nature of life, the preciousness of the moment, and the need for empathy for others' woes. Conversely, it serves as a point of comparison with, and therefore can help to intensify, contrasting feelings such as unbarred joy, elation, and delight. Finally, sadness can "go through the center" of ourselves, as Rilke put it in *Letters to a Young Poet*; it can bring something new, something life-altering. He goes on: "Were it possible for us to see further than our knowledge...perhaps we would endure our sadnesses with greater confidence than our joys. For they are the moments when something new has entered us, something unknown."

While *fear* diminishes and confines us, it also highlights that which towers over us. Certainly, fear can humiliate, but research suggests it also can sober us about what can and cannot be achieved. Fear acts as a backdrop for courage. Without fear courage would mean little and likely impact little in the course of our lives. Would we even seek to be courageous if we had no fear? Would we seek new fields, and fresh thoughts, sensations, or innovations without encountering some degree of fear? These questions are rarely asked by enthusiasts of so-called transhuman technologies.

Anger arouses danger, explosiveness, and domination. It is a fiery blast and an expansion that threatens decimation of others. But informed studies also show that anger is a way of standing up for oneself, as in righteous indignation; it is an impetus to courage and rejuvenation of spirit. Invigorating revolutions have upwelled from anger, and so have personal liberations. Without anger, tenderness may be thin, the poignancy of kindness unnoticed.

Coveting the qualities of another is the seedling of *envy*; obsessing over and fantasizing about possessing those qualities is the blossoming of envy. Envy arouses desperation to be something other than what one is; it is a maddening torment. But my experience as a therapist as well as client has shown me that envy is also an aspiration, a prospect, and a potentially life-changing breakthrough. We see the glimmers of our desires in those we envy and thereby have some capacity to nurture those desires. Envy contrasts with contentment and, by way of contrast, lends contentment its restorative depth.

Guilt alerts us to words or deeds we regret. It is a hammer in the depths of conscience and it pummels all forms of complacency. Guilt dims our acceptability and dashes our esteem. At the same time, as studies of psychopathy have shown, guilt and its social counterpart, shame, jar us to improve, apprise us of our potentiality to do better, and move us to heal others' wounds. It's hard to inspire change if we fail to encounter guilt.

The key to my own therapy, and indeed depth–existential therapy as a whole, is that it supports the coexistence of emotional and intellectual contraries. I loved and I hated at the same time. I was terrified of death, and yet I was intrigued by its mystery, by the mystery of life. I was jarred by scary movies and yet they opened me to alternative approaches to life, future possibilities, and my own imagination.

By emphasizing *presence*, depth–existential therapists make every effort to "hold" the contradictions that naturally arise in the course of their relationships with clients as well as within the clients themselves. In this way, depth–existential therapy becomes a staging ground for the humility and wonder, sense of adventure, and awe for living that is the hallmark of what we call a "whole bodied" transformation.

As a client in therapy myself, I have moved from positions of abject terror, to gradual intrigue, to wonder about my life circumstances. For example, I have shifted from paralysis before the unpredictability of fate, to incremental trust, curiosity, and fascination with what may be discovered. Through their abiding presence, my therapists supported me to feel safe enough to face my inner battle. They held a mirror for me to see close up both how I was currently living as well as how I *could* live should I gradually step out of my cramped yet familiar world. Back and forth I swung between terror and wonder and wonder back to terror, from quailing apprehension to incremental intrigue toward that which horrified, and from social withdrawal to growing risks with my therapists and the world at large.

The result was that after several years of therapy, I was able to experience the fuller ranges of my thoughts, feelings, and sensations. I, like many of the people I have worked with, was freed to attain goals but also greater presence to my life and to life itself. The result was that I became less identified with the old and crippling parts of life and more identified with the new and evolving parts, the parts that deeply mattered.

Personally, I practice what I call "existential–integrative" or EI, therapy, which coordinates a range of useful modalities under the existential approach (Schneider, 2015). As therapist, I am available to work with the patient at the most immediate, affective, kinesthetic, and profound level of contact possible.

For example, when I work with a patient I see myself more as a fellow traveler, as the existential analyst Irv Yalom put it, rather than the formal "doctor" serving up a remedy. I attempt to be available as a person rather than an engineer. I attune to the needs of my human patient, not to a bundle of electro-chemical processes or a diagnostic label. That doesn't mean I won't try to support that patient in whatever way may be helpful at the given time—for example, with a medical referral or a problem-solving strategy—but I will strive to be available to that patient to address the feelings, body sensations, and images behind the words and explanations.

All this involves attention to process, not just content. The approach supports a "whole bodied" awareness of both what the patient desires, as well as what blocks him or her from what is desired on the deepest of levels, often beyond words. In this way, any decision emerging from the therapy is energized by the whole body and that patient's visceral core.

Not every patient can or wants to work at the profound level of my integrative offering; but for those who do and can, the approach provides the chance for a life-changing shift. This shift bolsters one's capacity to experience the fuller ranges of one's thoughts, feelings, and sensations—one's whole bodily encounter with life. Based on that foundation, it's possible to make bold, concrete, meaningful changes in one's life. Put another way, such clients are able to cultivate a deep and abiding presence to themselves and the world, and through that presence to experience humility, wonder, and a sense of adventure toward living. This sense, for those who can really live it, fosters meaning, poignancy, and awe.

The reason we need such therapy today is precisely because the awe-based is too often left out of our programmatic, medicalized approaches to life. We assist people to change, but increasingly the impetus for that change is expedience: regulating our emotions, stopping negative thoughts, sleeping better at night, becoming more efficient, living more rationally, and so on. And while these therapeutic ends are by no means trifling, they are but "footholds" for many people along a broader and deeper path: the zest, meaning, and awe of being alive.

Cultivating the Life-Enhancing Anxiety of Awe:
Nineteen Practical Steps
Following are practical steps readers can take to enhance their
experience of awe toward life. These steps are drawn from my own
and others' paths over many years of grappling with life-enhancing
anxiety (see Schneider, 2009):

- Take time to reflect (be present)
- Develop a capacity to slow down
- Develop a capacity to savor the moment
- Focus on what one loves
- Practice seeing the big picture
- Cultivate openness to the mystery of life (including wonder
  and surprise)
- Cultivate an appreciation for the fact of life
- Foster an appreciation of pain as a sometime teacher
- Nurture an appreciation of balance (e.g., between fragility and
  boldness)
- Seek contemplative time alone
- Seek contemplative time in nature
- Pursue contemplative time with close others
- Travel
- Experience in-depth therapy or meditation[2]
- Find an awe-based mentor
- Cultivate an ability to trust the evolving nature of conflict (e.g.,
  "This too shall pass")
- Cultivate an ability to trust the evolving nature of life
- Nurture an ability to give oneself over—discerningly—to the
  unknowable
- Nurture an ability to trust the ultimately unknowable

---

[2] Exploration with psychedelics may also be a pathway to cultivating the life-enhancing
anxiety of awe. In my view, there needs to be more study of how such "therapies" affect
people over time and the extent to which they complement "natural" or non-drug-
assisted capacities to live awe-filled—fuller, richer—lives. Some of the recent
investigations in this area show promise (e.g., Pollan, 2018).

Part 2

Life-Enhancing Anxiety in the Arts

Overview

This section explores life-enhancing anxiety through film and classic works of literature. Although these works illuminate more through "showing" than "telling," as the great philosopher Ludwig Wittgenstein (2001) might have put it, they reveal the power of emotional learning over that which predominantly impacts our intellect. We begin with the cautionary tales of three soul-jarring films: *Antichrist, Melancholia*, and *Don't Look Up*. This chapter is then followed by a study of the extravagant in literature and life: *The Lure of Excess.*

Chapter 6

From Despair and Fanaticism to Awe: A Post-traumatic Growth Perspective on Cinematic Horror[1]

> "The poetry of transgression is also knowledge. He who transgresses…goes somewhere that others are not; and he learns something that others don't know."
> —Susan Sontag (2009)

Some fears run deeper than threats to life, limb, or property (although I don't make light of these). Some fears (or technically anxieties) are cosmic in nature and appear to underlie and yet elude our day-to-day realities.

The films I am about to discuss elucidate what H.P. Lovecraft (1973) terms *cosmic fear* and I term the *groundlessness* of being. By groundlessness of being, I mean the radically unknown, or in Rudolf Otto's (1923/1958) terms, "tremendous mystery" of creation. Groundlessness of being encompasses but also, in my view, exceeds death anxiety. While death anxiety is conventionally associated with the demise of a living organism, groundlessness is associated with the underlying oblivion or shattering of identity that accompanies such demise (e.g., see Kohut, 1977 on "disintegration anxiety"). While we "know" something about how an organism dies (e.g., the physical processes of deterioration), we know virtually nothing about the post-death identity of that organism. It is this dissolution of identity into the void of space–time, or the threat of such dissolution, that I call "groundlessness."

In *Horror and the Holy: Wisdom-teachings of the Monster Tale* (Schneider, 1993), I showed how this groundlessness or infinity of

---

[1] Author's Note: This chapter is adapted from an essay in *Death in Classic and Contemporary Film* (2013, pp. 217–229) edited by Jeff Greenberg and Daniel Sullivan. New York: Palgrave Macmillan.

being infuses some of the most compelling horror classics ever created and is precisely the basis for their captivation. I also showed how this groundlessness is associated with constrictive or expansive endlessness or the uncontained. Allusion to these phenomena are vividly animated in such classics as *Frankenstein* (1931), *Dracula* (1931), *Phantom of the Opera* (1925), *Dr. Jekyll and Mr. Hyde* (1932), *Vertigo* (1958), and *Alien* (1979); but such allusions can also be seen throughout the horror genre as a whole as illustrated, for example, by the occultism in *The Exorcist* (1973) or the explosiveness in *Halloween* (1978).

That said, the most striking feature of the groundlessness theme in these films was not just its horror but its wonder. By wonder, I mean the curiosity, fascination, and even amazement evoked by the groundlessness of being. For example, consider the implication of death transcendence in *Frankenstein*, or mind-reading in *Dracula*, or contagion in *Alien*. Each of these are exhilarating as much as they are hair-raising and present opportunities to radically transform lives. And yet there is a problem in each of these (cautionary) tales; they do not highlight the exhilarating! Indeed, they highlight the monstrous, which requires some reflection.

In my own study of the structure of classic horror, I found that a very intriguing pattern emerges that emulates real-life dilemmas on many levels. This pattern is what I call the "traumatic cycle" of classic horror, and it proceeds as follows: An innocent protagonist, such as a Dr. Frankenstein or Count Dracula, encounters an agonizing tragedy, such as the death of Dr. Frankenstein's mother in childbirth or the slaughter of a tribe in the case of Count Dracula. This traumatic shock or jolt then catapults the protagonist into a dark despair, which renders their feeling both hopeless and helpless. But this despair is not just ordinary disconsolation: It is screaming, foundation-shaking disconsolation, or what I call *cosmic* in scale.

Consider, for example, the experience of pain in the lives of Victor Frankenstein and Count Dracula or, for that matter, Erik the Phantom (who was burned as a youth), or Dr. Jekyll (who was crushed by Victorian values), or Scottie, the detective in *Vertigo*, who lost his partner to a fatal fall, or just about any of the other protagonists in classic horror: These are dysphorias of a monumental nature, because, if one really dwells upon it, all great losses are of a monumental nature. All great losses shake us, pulverize us, and make us realize the fragility of our position—and not just as individuals in a body and culture, but as creatures in a cosmos and void. They make us realize that we are all in suspense on this tiny orb of life, and that the "base" or "ground" that holds us in this suspense is no base or ground at all; it is a vacuum (Schneider, 2009, 2013).

Hence the sense of *cosmic helplessness* is a real and pervasive substrate of virtually any human suffering, and classic horror illuminates this problem with profundity. But classic horror does something else; it wakes us up to the potential consequences of such helplessness, which can be equally devastating. These consequences ensue when unprocessed trauma (despair) leads to unprocessed defense, and this defense takes the form of rage, fanaticism, and ultimately monstrosity. Hence, monstrosity (or fanaticism) is the second part of the traumatic cycle of horror. The fury of Dr. Frankenstein's grim efforts to extend life, or Count Dracula's drive to overtake life, or Mr. Hyde's striving to absorb life are all examples of this fanatical stage of reaction.

In the third and final stage of the traumatic cycle, there is a glimmer of what I formerly called wonder—and I now term *awe*—in the trajectory of monstrous protagonists. This wonder or awe is more often implied than explicit in classic horror—consider, for example, the physiological complexity of the Frankenstein monster or the emotional intricacy of Count Dracula—but nevertheless it is palpable, accessible, and even inspirational. I now use the term "awe" rather than "wonder" for this third stage of the traumatic cycle because I have come to believe in its superior accuracy, depth, and relevance to actual experience (Schneider, 2004, 2009). By awe, I mean the comingling of wonder and anxiety, vulnerability and humility. I also mean the sense of adventure associated with the extraordinary and even the monstrous. In short, I define this third stage of awe as the humility and wonder—or sense of adventure—within horrific imagery. Note that I am not equating awe with the horrific, but in keeping with the tone of classic films, I am citing the *potential* for an awesome experience *within and perhaps even as a result of* the original horrific calamity.

From a psychological standpoint, this third stage could also be viewed as a stage of *post-traumatic growth* (Tedeschi & Calhoun, 1995). This stage refers to the potential for a deepening and enlargement of consciousness in the aftermath of trauma (or horror). This potential for growth, moreover, is in my view integral to the structure of classic horror. Such horror, in other words, operates not only at the level of scaring and titillating viewers but also at the level of alerting them to alternative universes, remarkable states of mind, and astounding conditions of embodiment. The caveat here, however, is that such illumination can only proceed if the traumatic basis for the horror can be faced, deliberated upon, and in some viable sense worked through—which is precisely what the protagonists in classic horror rarely do! The onus for such a working through must of necessity then fall to us, the horror viewership. While the writer of the screenplay may provide us hints, it is up to us to reconceive these hints and indeed to reconceive the trajectory of classic horror itself. What this trajectory will ultimately look like is anyone's guess, but it will likely encompass the awe that is implicit in the monstrosity or, to put it more plainly, the awe dimension *between* fanaticism and despair. Consider, for example, if Victor Frankenstein or Scottie (the protagonist in *Vertigo*) for that matter, had perceived their disabilities as a chance for new and vibrant lives rather than desperate lunges for the unattainable.

In the balance of this chapter, I will show how two contemporary films elucidate the traumatic cycle discussed above. I will show further how these films elucidate major challenges in the real contemporary world and the prospects for a redress to these challenges.

The two films I will illustrate are Lars von Trier's *Antichrist* (2009) and *Melancholia* (2011)—films that in my estimation, epitomize the despair, fanaticism, and awe of our contemporary world. Like Hitchcock before him, von Trier is a master at cutting through life's surfaces and exposing the abysses below; he is also a master at depicting people's relationships to those abysses in the contemporary world, and this is where his work bears relevance to the present discussion.

Finally, I will present a more recent film—*Don't Look Up* (2021)—that provides a coda or update on how despair, fanaticism, and awe play out in certain quarters of today's world. Although *Don't Look Up* is most reflective of the *Melancholia* theme, it mirrors the more general lament in both *Melancholia* and *Antichrist* about the loss of life-enhancing anxiety and its implication for a grave loss of our humanity.

Antichrist

Antichrist is a merciless film. By that I mean that it does not merely critique but "sledgehammers" contemporary Western values. The film opens with "Lascia ch'io pianga," the music from Handel's *Rinaldo*, and from there marches straight into our solar plexus. The opening scene is a tone poem of operatic sublimity and domestic serenity, as a young couple gracefully ease into lovemaking while their toddler, Nic, playfully climbs up toward the windowsill in an adjacent room. By depicting the events in slow motion, the scene achieves an eeriness that matches its intensity. As the couple deepens their passionate conjugation, the camera quickly pans over to Nic. Nic hesitates at first but innocently edges toward the open window to improve his view of the beckoning outdoors (where it is both snowing and radiant). Just as the couple achieves climactic bliss, von Trier guides the viewer's eye once again to Nic. But this time Nic is not climbing; he is spiraling, wide-eyed and obliviously to his grizzly death.

When the couple discovers this abomination, they are racked by self-incrimination and guilt. The presumed mother (played by Charlotte Gainsbourg) expresses this guilt by psychically imploding, and the presumed father (played by Willem Defoe) deals with it by quickly and vehemently occupying his professional role as a therapist. That he is concertedly a cognitive–behavioral therapist is made conspicuously evident in the succeeding scenes.

The mother's internal shattering begins with a primeval withdrawal that becomes the center of her husband's rescue-obsessed world. It should be said at the outset that as a viewer, one cannot help but empathize with these people. Their son was killed by a seemingly random accident. On the other hand, the situation, like so many in von Trier's vision, is riddled with ambiguity. The couple could have prevented the calamity—had they secured the window that ushered the boy's death. They could have kept a closer eye on him as parents are wont to do with toddlers, and so on. But still, there is nothing that exceeds comprehension in the evolution of this scenario, and at this point in the film there is no one who is unequivocally responsible. Add that to the juxtaposition of the boy's demise with the couple's ecstatic lovemaking and you have one of the most harrowing convergence of scenes in cinematic history.

The father tries virtually everything from his cognitive–behavioral toolbox to calm, cajole, and contain his partner's darkening despair—and virtually nothing works (including a surfeit of psychiatric drugs). The mother, meanwhile, spirals ever deeper into grief, guilt, and agitation. The father is also clearly impacted, but he is much more adept than the mother at curtailing himself, and, to the outside observer at least, appears much the healthier of the pair. But appearances are deceiving in this enigmatic work, and tables begin to turn.

In time, the mother's cascade into helplessness acquires an angry, rageful quality that is both confusing and disturbing to the father. After a particularly futile period, the father decides to help the mother by employing exposure therapy to recondition her associations to the calamity. Ground zero for this exposure experiment is a country retreat, ironically called "Eden," they have shared through the years. The father hoped that by pairing relaxation responses with the scene of his partner's most dreaded nightmare—the cabin retreat where she and Nic spent some of their most intimate moments—she would begin to form new and more stable cognitive associations.

But strange things begin to happen when they arrive at the place. The father, for example, is confronted by a bizarre deer; as the deer turns to leave, a bloodied fawn hangs from its womb. More puzzlements follow: As the mother heads further into her terror, acorns start pelting the cabin windows, ticks start to invade the father's hand, and a bizarre self-mutilating fox utters the words "chaos reigns." And indeed, chaos is the watchword for the evolving scenario, as the couple is further immersed in their bewilderment. This state of affairs is especially devastating to the father—guardian of order and reason—and von Trier pulls no punches in depicting this.

In a subsequent scene, the father discovers his wife's doctoral thesis on witch hunts of the 17th century buried in the basement shelves. To his chagrin, this thesis reveals not only her fascination with these campaigns but the conclusion that they were *justified.* So here we have an intelligent, thoroughly contemporary woman who methodically arrives at the conclusion that women are indeed evil. How can that happen, von Trier seems to query. Further, the mother begs her husband to hit her during sex. He reluctantly agrees in an outdoor scene underneath a large tree. As the couple makes love, a multitude of hands emerges from the roots of the tree.

Later, the father discovers that Nic's feet were deformed, as shown in his autopsy photo—this deformation apparently had no relation to his fatal fall and had almost the quality of something unworldly. The deformation takes an even more perverted turn as the mother, upon discovering it, turns wild and realizes that she was the only one with Nic at the time the deformation apparently first became evident. Inexplicably, she loses all inhibition at this point and begins to attack the husband. At first this attack takes a sexual form but shockingly, in one of the most agonizing moments on film, she grabs a block of wood and smashes it into her husband's groin. This precipitates a frantic and blood-spewing fight for survival in which both perpetrator and victim, predator and prey, alternate in a maddening spin into anarchy. The husband is now about as far away from psychological professionalism as one can get, and the wife has completely shattered the traditional role of femininity (including committing gynocide, or the mutilation of female genitalia, on herself!). No convention is safe at this point, and the primal terrors of nature abound. But it is more than primal terror, as that term is typically understood. It is also otherworldly terror, and it upends every "law" in its path.

In the penultimate scene, the father frees himself from a horrific grindstone that his wife has somehow drilled into his leg. Yes, I said "drilled." In his scramble for survival, the father ends up strangling the mother and escapes into the woods. The final scene, which is perhaps the most enigmatic, shows the father staggering through the woods. As he reaches a hillside he is swarmed by legions of ghostly women who "dance" with him into a valley below.

Analysis
There is no definitive analysis of *Antichrist*, and it is one of the most enigmatic films of the last 20 years. However, from the standpoint of this chapter, several aspects of the film are clear. First, the film unquestionably anatomizes despair. From the opening scene of annihilation, despair is imbued in the faces and mannerisms of the protagonist parents. Although the mother's behavior is most explicitly despairing, it is clear (at least to this observer) that the father is equally distraught but quickly finds a diversionary strategy. This strategy, which is almost ingrained in his character, is cognitive–behavioral psychology, science, and ultimately the supremacy of reason. Another way to look at this supremacy of reason is in accord with the masculine principle of Jungian psychology. This principle emphasizes order, containment, and control (Jung, 1966). Further, it is clear that in *Antichrist*, the masculine principle is concertedly set against the equally tenacious female principle, symbolized by the more than passing reference to chaos amid various scenes; "chaos reigns," as the fox betokens. In Babylonian lore, chaos is represented by the Goddess Tiamat, the source of all being.

Beyond these Jungian associations, however, the upshot of the film is conspicuously existential: There is no supremacy, there are no simple answers, and there is no unequivocal truth, at least among sentient beings. Von Trier characterized *Antichrist* as a "scream" (Schwarzbaum, 2009), and that is precisely what it is—on multiple levels. It is a scream at the randomness of fate, a scream at the frailty of youth, a scream at the betrayal of life, and a scream at those who deny the scream. The father, like so much of contemporary society, denied the scream itself and in so doing turned his back on life. Life cannot be powerful if it is unworthy of a scream; and when life ceases to have power it becomes a vacuum.

The vacuum in the father's case led to a kind of crazed rationality, a monstrosity of formulation—that oppressed every fiber of his own and his wife's need to grieve. While he could tolerate this stultification of natural life processes, at least for a time, his wife could not. Her pain was a whirlwind, and like the shadows and inexplicabilities of her son's death, it could not be brooked. To that extent it cracked and then shattered the pretensions of order as offered by her husband, and opened wildly to the frontier. The more she denied that frontier, the more vigorously a part of herself rebelled and yielded to it.

In the latter half of the film, the frontier becomes all-consuming as the father's artifice could hold for only so long. Soon, his oppression of her breaks out into her oppression of him, and the monstrosities of them both break out in all directions. Thus, it is here that we arrive at the nub of the film. The "antichrist," in my view, stands for all positions that polarize, that demonize, and that privilege a single vantage point to the utter exclusion of competing vantage points. The antichrist is the fanatical rationality and reductionism of the demoralized father; it is the volcanic backlash and sadism of the mother; and it is the unchecked fury and shadow side of nature when debased.

The point here is that the father, and by implication Western society, "manages" reality at their peril. No one is clean and neat, and no historical period can be summarily dismissed. For example, while we expected that the mother's doctoral thesis would excoriate the hateful torturers of witches, the opposite occurred. When a cabin in the woods looked tame and undefiled, it turned out to be anything but. And when the father's studied and professional manner appeared constructive, it got turned on its head. What this amounts to is that no professional, no doctor, no feminist, and no contemporary pundit can arrogantly place themselves above the complexities of the world and simply declare their truth as *the* truth.

So what is the concluding message of the film? I think it is something like this: The best we humans can offer is a heartfelt and mindful response to, rather than reaction against, our tragic condition. For example, if the father had engaged his own grief, acknowledged its power, and gradually discovered its capacity to transform, he may have supported his wife to grieve in kind. Correspondingly, if the wife had been able to gain more insight into managing her own grief, as well as her husband's defenses against it, she may have supported both of them to process rather than simply react against their abject despair.

Through this processing, the couple may still have experienced nightmares (indeed, they assuredly would experience nightmares), but they would be woven into a tapestry of possibilities rather than a monolithic extreme; they would be more nuanced fears rather than black-and-white terrors.

The dance with the ghostly women at the end of the film may well have represented the dance the father—as well as mother—rarely permitted themselves: that is, a dance with being, in all its stark reality, all its radiance and renewal. "You must have chaos within you," observed Nietzsche (1960), "in order to give birth to a dancing star" (p. 9). The "antichrist" of the film, I contend, was precisely this inability to dance, precisely the destruction wrought by the fixed positions of the protagonists.

Melancholia

The pretensions to modernity, to fashion, and to our technocratic age are no less in focus in von Trier's latest meditation on mortality—*Melancholia* (2011). From the outset, *Melancholia* is bathed in foreboding. Yet one can hardly overestimate the mixtures of pain and beauty, pathos and elegance in this opening sequence. With the exception of one wonder-struck woman, faces are tortured, bodies are scurrying, and a slow-motion haze is cast over a lavish, disintegrating order. The disintegration on the ground is juxtaposed with an eerily graceful sky. Slowly a glowing orb emerges into this sky, and by the end of this deranged yet fascinating sequence the orb plunges into the planet on which the mayhem has broken out. That planet is Earth.

In the next scene, we wind the reel back, and a couple, looking like they just leaped out of the pages of *Vanity Fair*, become stranded on the way to their wedding. The woman, Justine (played by Kirsten Dunst), is dressed like an angel, and the man, Michael (played by Alexander Skarsgård), is tellingly non-descript. When their cab gets stuck in the mud, it is Justine, not Michael, who maneuvers their way out.

When the couple arrives at their party (an enormous estate filled with anxiously awaiting guests), they are greeted by Justine's sister, Claire (Charlotte Gainsbourg), along with her husband, John (Kiefer Sutherland). Claire appears rather "buttoned down" compared with her freewheeling and volatile sister, and John is every bit the contemporary aristocrat, gracious yet arrogant behind the benign veneer.

Following some tense and awkward toasts from the attendees, particularly those of the sisters' parents, Justine begins to unravel. First this unraveling shows up in her indifference toward her betrothed, but then it becomes more encompassing, as if the whole ill-fated celebration was her adversary. John's arrogance, her father's infantilism, her mother's embitterment, her boss's narrow and petty entitlement, and her sister's rigidity, all begin driving Justine deeper into her despair, and, resultantly, her authentic life. Following her vacant sexual responses to Michael, Justine communes naked with the moonlight. She finds a lover on one of these escapades and communes equivalently with him. Increasingly, she grows alienated. The world of phony talk, cardboard personalities, and pedantic aspirations no longer sustains her.

In a word, Justine goes *mad*. But this madness, as we soon grasp, is not simple chemical imbalance or emotional derangement. It is the madness of insight and widening view. It is the madness commemorated in *Hamlet* and *King Lear*, and that inquirers such as R.D. Laing (1967) have touted as "potential breakthroughs" as well as breakdowns. The emerging fact is that Justine can *see* more of what's going on than virtually anyone else in her environment, and this drives her into paralytic depression but also correspondingly penetrating visions about the conditions of humanity.

It is useful at this point to again show how trenchant von Trier can be in his metaphorical critique of contemporary culture. John and the party-goers can be seen as the "cheerful robots" of the happiness age (see also Becker, 1974). These denizens are all reflexive and driven, the unwitting victims of Madison Avenue manipulators and Establishment hacks. The only clear thinker is the madwoman who cuts through the glitter, the woman who, in professional parlance, is a "depressive realist" and who "ranges over the wider scale of experience" than her supposedly adjusted contemporaries (Alloy & Abramson, 1988; James, 1902/1936, p. 160).

Just what Justine perceives in this world is telling. It is a world that is on a crash course, a world that is about to collide with another world—the planet Melancholia—that is in its path. But she sees much more; she sees that the world has always been wobbly and yet blind often to its predicament. She sees a world that has hunkered down into fiefdoms, treated them as universes, and denied the majesty of its bearing.

John, her sister's impeccably dressed husband, has all the latest gadgetry, all the best cars, and all the latest furnishings. He is an amateur astronomer and makes it a point to teach his young son Leo all about the latest findings of astronomical import. But the main finding he focuses on is Melancholia, and with the assurance of so many today, he conveys with great confidence the "facts" his scientific brethren share. These facts are as follows: Melancholia is a fluke planet. It took our detection devices by surprise, but it is not a threat to our planet. John absorbs this clap-trap like gospel and cheerily goes about spreading it to whomever is within earshot.

Justine, on the other hand, is the artist–seer who does not simply accept the received word. She looks mad to a madly ordered world because she is in touch with the actual madness that the world denies— life's fragility. She's also in touch with what she calls the "evil" of this world, but it is not evil in some moralizing sense. In my view, it is the evil of not recognizing the groundlessness of our condition, and the cover-ups—wars, fanaticisms, and fantasy systems—that are its consequences (Schneider, 2013). Yet as much as the groundlessness of our condition can be a terrifying problem, it can also be freeing and ennobling—particularly if it moves us to appreciate here–now life. And this is precisely what Justine seeks, or attempts to seek, when she's not thwarted by personal or cultural fetters.

As the planets come closer and Claire's anxiety rises, Justine interestingly becomes calm. This shift makes much sense in a world where denial begins to give way to consciousness, and the "sane" become more discomfited. Justine and Claire in fact begin to switch roles with one another, with Justine assuming caretaking responsibilities and Claire beginning to fray. As John becomes aware that his calculations are bogus—as with much that he has staked his life on—he, too, begins breaking apart. This disintegration culminates in his suicide, which is conspicuously situated in the stall of one of his horses. It is as if the message is that the fanatical human is more perishable than the horse, for the horse, much like the evolving Justine, has become calm by this point in the film, attuned to and accepting of his fate.

Following John's death, Justine takes an increasingly maternal role with both Claire and Leo. The question now becomes: How will they respond to the oncoming disaster? Claire conjures up a half-baked plan for the three of them to share a drink at the moment of collision, but Justine rejects this plan in seeming deference to the needs of Leo. In the next scene, Justine is seen embracing Leo as they peer out into the menacing world. The boy understandably is in terror, and invokes his dad's worst-case calculations: My dad says that if the planets collide there will be nothing left, he states in effect. Then Justine calmly turns to him and says, "Well, if your dad says that, then he didn't know about the magic cave."

In the final scene Justine, Claire, and Leo are seen constructing the magic cave. This "cave," a tent-like structure made of sticks and twine, is designed to shelter them from the oncoming chaos. Whether it does or not is beside the point. The closing scene portrays Justine and Leo calmly huddling, and Claire wincing as the apocalypse strikes.

Analysis

Kierkegaard once said that the "best an individual can attain" is "objective uncertainty, held fast, in the most personal passionate experience" (cited in Tillich, 1963). This is another way of saying that we cannot know anything for certain, but we can choose our response to events, and that response can be personal, passionate, and far-ranging. In *Melancholia*, Justine chose a Kierkegaardian response to her and the world's fate. She chose to opt out of the petty games and artificial ploys of conventional society to embrace a world of depth, enigma, and wonder. She chose a response to the demise of that world (our world) that draws on the greatest freedom we possess—our imagination. No one is to say whether such imagination is ultimately "real" or "valid." But what one can say is that like Sisyphus with his rock, Justine engaged the best and last freedom with which a human is endowed, and she shared it with a child.

Claire and the rest of the wedding guests could do none of the above. Imagination had long ago been boxed out of their world. As a result they exhibited one of two basic reactions: either abject despair, as when Claire and John recognized the undeniability of the oncoming *Melancholia*, or fanaticism, as when Claire and John fostered the pretense of their "higher" nature either through propriety, fashion, or technology. Whereas Justine also had her desperate and fanatical reactions, they were not primarily to *Melancholia*. They were to the pretenses that so much of the world had erected to deny *Melancholia*, and by implication, all the lesser melancholias that contemporary culture strives to cordon off. She became an incorrigible depressive or provocateur to preserve herself and break free. But she did not become stuck in these polarities, and this is what distinguished her from her more entrenched peers. She somehow found the courage to battle with herself and the seduction of the quick fix or simple answer, and through that find a middle, deliberative path. While this path did not "solve" anything ultimately, it did enable her to wonder, to marvel, and to share her "inner-sight" with those whom she loved.

Summary and Conclusion

This essay anatomized despair, fanaticism, and awe in two classics of contemporary cinema. Like Hitchcock and Tarkovsky before him, von Trier has pointed to a new mythos for the emerging age. This mythos embraces neither rigid timidity nor explosive grandiosity in the face of cosmic bewilderment. By contrast, it offers an awe-based medicament that is both humbling and wondrous, savoring and adventurous in the moment-to-moment exercise of living. Short of that, the filmmakers imply, life devolves into monstrosity or, worse, no life at all.

Coda: *Don't Look Up*

Melancholia has been given a new life recently with the wildly popular film *Don't Look Up* (2021). *Don't Look Up* is like a comical *Melancholia*. But it is also a serious and important film, that goes straight for the jugular when it comes to anxiety denial. Just as in *Melancholia*, the comet in *Don't Look Up* is loaded with metaphors, which are now considerably weightier than the metaphors alluded to when *Melancholia* was produced. The stakes are even higher now, as is the destructive potential, and *Don't Look Up* makes both starkly evident.

Don't Look Up begins with a group of graduate students at Michigan State University. These students specialize in astrophysics and are led by a spirited professor—Dr. Mindy (played by Leonardo DiCaprio). One of Dr. Mindy's astute charges, Ph.D. candidate Kate Dibiasky (played by Jennifer Lawrence), happens to observe a five-to-ten-kilometer comet headed straight for Earth. The projected time of impact: six months.

When Dr. Mindy realizes the validity of Kate's finding, he calls on her to assist him in conveying the seriousness of this situation to government scientists, who then rather derisively refer them to the White House. Soon after, Dr. Mindy and Kate are invited to a meeting with the U.S. president (played by Meryl Streep) and her chief of staff. What then unfolds is a series of appalling yet tragically plausible dismissals of the two researchers and their message. This dismissal is not only perpetrated by the president and her chief of staff but by media outlets and the populace worldwide. People simply refuse to "see" or "hear" the gravity of Kate and Dr. Mindy's findings, and they are reinforced in their denial by media and computer gurus such as Brie Evantee, an entertainment reporter (played by Cate Blanchett), and Peter Isherwell, a Steve Jobs/Timothy Leary-like figure (played by Mark Rylance). The latter in particular are fanatically devoted to keeping life light, easy, and emotionally remote: Brie through her inane yet glib commentary as an infotainment host, along with her equally hollow co-host Jack Bremmer (played by Tyler Perry), and Peter as a kind of computer mastermind who believes that algorithms and profit margins will "save" civilization.

The irony, of course, is that none of these gimmicks prove effective in eradicating the comet, which furiously proceeds on its inexorable path. Only a handful of people—Dr. Mindy and Kate among them—seem capable of breaking out of the simplistic delusions promoted by the scions of contemporary culture, but only after faltering a few times. The desperation for speed, instant results, and surface answers in this world is mind-numbing, and anxiety is public enemy number one. Even the social outcasts such as Yule (played by Timothee Chalamet) are caught in the denial culture, albeit through different means such as intoxication and apathy, and the post-modern cacophony of today's world becomes palpably evident. It's as if the movie cries out: "How many forms of anxiety denial are out there today? Let us name them: denial through indifference, through drugs, through happiness, through food addiction, through smartphones, through computers, through military weaponry, through strong-arm leaders, through entertainers, through sports idols, through virtual relationships, through religious dogmas, through social status, through extremist ideologies, through racism, and through sexism, to name a few. And what is sacrificed in the wake of such preoccupations? The oncoming "comets" of climate change, pandemics, strong-arm dictatorships, civil and political upheaval, ethnic calamities, religious clashes, clashes over water rights, poverty, and inequality, to name a few. Oh, and also the humility and wonder, sense of awe toward life—the cherishing of life.

"So how are we going to respond to all this escapism, this superficiality and delusion?" the movie further implores. While Dr. Mindy, Kate and several others recognize the value of life-enhancing anxiety; it is too little and too late. Still, if there is a hopeful note in the film, it is in the cosmic reminder before they are all plowed under that "We really did have everything, didn't we?"

Chapter 7

The Lure of Excess in Life and Art[1]

This chapter anatomizes the experience of violence. Drawing on the phenomenological observations of classic literature and, in particular, the horror genre, this chapter proposes that the tendency toward violence is a complex, multifaceted phenomenon. While brain pathology, genetic disposition, and quantifiable stressors all appear to play a role in the outbreak of violence, the literary genre points to other, less well appreciated dimensions. Among these are: a sense of emptiness, the need to compensate for that emptiness through extreme and dramatic acts, and a lack of the sense of awe, meaning, and the carnivalesque in people's lives. This chapter argues for the restoration of awe, meaning, and the carnivalesque, not only as a hedge against the kind of violence observed in catastrophic outbreaks such as 9/11 and the recent war in Ukraine, but as a virtue in its own right, and as an antidote, comparatively, to our desolate times.

While it is obvious why people are repelled by violence—physical pain, emotional suffering, degradation, lack of control—in this chapter I anatomize a much subtler challenge: that which attracts us to violence. If we can throw light on this problem, we are well on our way to ameliorating it, to taking steps, both psychological and social, to minimizing its source.

What makes people risk lives, families, reputations, friendships, and personal freedom just to knock somebody down, maim, rape, or even kill? What prompted Mohamed Attah, the ringleader of the 9/11 ambush, to coolly and cruelly leave "instructions" about how to massacre 3,000 people?

The theories run from the physiological to the mental and emotional. Think, for example, about the influence of genetic disposition (the "bad seed" theory), brain damage, and hormonal imbalances; or consider the

---

[1] Author's Note: This chapter is adapted from "The Lure of Excess," published in the American Psychological Association Division 32 journal, *The Humanistic Psychologist*, Vol. 30, 274–280, 2002.

impact of childhood trauma, abuse, neglect, impoverishment, cultural alienation, and hostile/critical parenting or some combination of physiological and psychological factors. Most of these theories, however, derive from rather detached and analytical investigations—lab studies or naturalistic observation by trained social scientists. Not that this situation is bad. Such data do have their uses and help society make a variety of public policy decisions. But the problem is that such data are constricted in certain ways. They derive their conclusions from within the confines of traditional science (or empiricism), and this traditional framework only legitimates that which is overt and measurable; that which is affective, intuitive, and qualitative is left in abeyance.

The existential–phenomenological investigator, by contrast, is not hemmed in by such criteria. Their subject is the lifeworld, the pretheoretical, everyday understanding of the person or phenomenon before them, and their means of explicating the lifeworld is the rich and symbolic realm of language. The question for the existential phenomenologist, as it was for Becker (1973), is what (in its fullest possible sense) is the *experience* of violence? For example, in addition to asking what it means for others to experience violence, the existential–phenomenological investigator asks what it means for *me* (the investigator) to have the experience.

In the balance of this chapter, I will take this existential-phenomenological approach to violence. I will explore how violence is lived and embodied, not just reported on or measured. In particular, I am going to consider the lived attraction to violence as it is illustrated in classic horror tales, which I researched for my book *Horror and the Holy* (Schneider, 1993). While these tales parallel many of Becker's concerns about violence, I believe they go beyond them in certain ways and help to complement them.

What then do we learn from the horror genre about violence, and, in particular, the lure of violence? First, we learn that violence is typically an extreme or polarization of human experience. And like all extremes, violence is radical change, alteration. Think here of the radical change exhibited by Frankenstein's monster when he is rejected by the villagers: "I gave vent to my anguish in fearful howlings," the monster declares. "I bore a hell within me." "I was like a wild beast," "wished to tear up the trees, spread havoc and destruction." I "declared everlasting war against the [human] species" (Shelley, 1818/1981, p.121). This passage reminds me of the Blake quote from Proverbs of Hell: "The wrath of the lion is the wisdom of God. The roaring of lions, the howling of wolves, the raging of the stormy sea, and the destructive sword, are portions of eternity too great for the eye of man." I think here also of that magnificent scene where King Kong, on display in a huge cage in front of a vast urban crowd, breaks the chains and bars that bind him. Or what about the early scenes in the Fredric March version of *Jekyll & Hyde* (1932), where Hyde bursts out of his laboratory, pushes his face into the driving rain, and runs about London throwing everyone out of his way. Then there is that remarkable scene in Hitchcock's *Vertigo* (1958) where Scotty, played by Jimmy Stewart, is hanging by the gutter of a skyscraper peering into the depths below. Violence can take more subtle forms as well: the image of the invisible man terrorizing a village or the phantom of the opera trapping his victims in the dreaded Palace of Mirrors, or Dracula penetrating a young nubile with his menacing fangs or paralyzing someone with his piercing eyes. Take a moment to consider your favorite scenes from classic horror. What intrigues you about these scenes? What transfixes you?

I think you would concur that these images carry with them a degree of titillation and excitement as well as horror and disgust. Why is this? My own provisional conclusion is that violence—extremism, monstrosity— is an ultimate manifestation of the alterations that bring us joy and even ecstasy; that in many cases what we call violence is simply the unrestrained and unmanageable outcropping of what we call joy, release, liberation. I am not alone in this observation. Witness the words of the great craftsman of horror H.P. Lovecraft (1973): "Yet who shall declare the dark theme a positive handicap? Radiant with beauty, the cup of the Ptolemies was carven of onyx" (p. 106). Or hearken to this breathtaking summation by Susan Sontag (2009): "The poetry of transgression is also knowledge. He who transgresses not only breaks a rule. He goes somewhere that others are not; and he knows something that the others don't know."

Stated more formally, I believe that violence is attractive precisely because it is associated with the enlargement of consciousness (mental and physical agitation, upheaval, boundary breaking). In some cases, such as the creation of a Frankenstein figure, violence is associated with the farthest, least bearable consciousness that we can attain—to wit, the resurrection of the flesh as in the biblical story of Lazarus. (Recall the scene where Jesus raises Lazarus in Scorcese's *Last Temptation of Christ*). This thesis may sound strange coming from an ostensibly kind and thoughtful student of psychology, but I genuinely believe it reflects the facts. The further we extend and enlarge ourselves, the more our experience appears bizarre, unassimilable, and, in many cases, perverse and violent—just as nature and the cosmos appear perverse and violent at their extremes.

Given this understanding, however, I am not saying that violence is good or that we should in some sense strive for it. This would be a total misreading of my thesis. What I am saying is that there is something animating, growthful, and inspiriting within violence that violent people, in their own misguided way, strive to engage (consider Rollo May's (1969) notion of the "daimonic" or Burke's (1757/1998) view of the "sublime."). I view violence, in other words, as an overcompensation that blindly and compulsively overshoots its aim. Victor Frankenstein, for example, intended to enhance human life, to strengthen and extend such life, but he was so driven, so blindly obsessed with that aim (due to his past state of unstrength and existential helplessness) that he went overboard and created a mockery of his desire. Other madmen and monsters in horror classics experience similar compensatory transformations. They "meddle in things men should leave alone," as one character put it in *The Invisible Man* (1933), or they "trespass on God's domain" as it was put in the film *Jekyll and Hyde*. We are not too far afield, moreover, when we compare these figures in horror stories to the legions of real monstrosities and abusers in the world; for they, too, generally suffer from impotencies and impoverishments of all sorts. And they, too, blindly and reflexively hyperreact to these conditions, becoming extremists, berzerkers, and fanatics as a result. Recall the interview with mass murderer Jeffrey Dahmer where he talked about the unbarred power he experienced while planning and carrying out his cannibalistic acts. Or take Attah again. It may not be too much of a stretch to consider that whatever else was driving this incendiary zealot, such as religious principles and cultural estrangement, his own inner fragility, and the quest to stanch it, was a major factor. According to a *New York Times* article, Attah was shamed incessantly as a child and his vulnerability and "girlishness" mocked (Robin, 2001).

Even we the audience or witnesses, then, can get caught up in the morbid fascinations of real-life monstrosities. And even we, the "innocents," can resonate with or even entertain similar fascinations within ourselves (recall Hitler's Germany or Stalin's Russia). And yet such fascinations are crucial because they are the key, I believe, to getting at the roots of the problem of violence. Specifically, too many are fascinated by violence today because our society is bereft of the components that many of us, as well as violent people, misguidedly seek—a sense of awe, a sense of wonder, and a sense of spiritual sustenance. Each of these dimensions has been systematically eroded in our society over the past several centuries. Each has been eclipsed by growing needs for industrialization, be it capitalistic or communistic, or, on the other hand, in the context of the rising interests of fundamentalist religions, theocracies. It's difficult, if not impossible, to cultivate awe and wonder—*life-enhancing anx*iety—where there is little freedom, where time is held hostage, or where personal expression is stifled. (See the book *Jihad vs. McWorld* by Benjamin Barber, 1995.)

What then, can we do about this dire state of affairs? How can we create conditions whereby people feel more fulfilled, less panicked, and less driven to evolve monstrous forms of overcompensation? While there are obviously no simple answers to this question, the metaphor of *carnival* has been of increasing help to me in my exploration of the issue. By carnival I mean a certain kind of spirit, a spirit, as Richard Rorty (1991) discussed in his essay on Heidegger, Kundera, and Dickens, that embodies play, adventure, complexity, and compassion (see also Mikhail Bakhtin's [1984] incredible *Rabelais and His World*). Rorty traces this spirit to the legacy left to us by Western literary traditions—the works of such greats as Dante, Cervantes, Goethe, Dickens and, I might add, that of such authors of classic horror as Shelley, Stoker, and Stevenson.

An infusion of carnival (which literally means raising or celebrating the flesh, coming alive) would be salutary to our world. The great question, of course, is how do we go about incorporating carnival in today's regimented climate? While I greatly struggle with this question, I do have some thoughts on the matter (see also Schneider, 1999). First, our entire socio-economic system has to be reformed. We need to aim much less at material acquisition, wealth, status, and industrialization, and much more at cultivating meaning, purpose, and adventure in our lives. We must, in other words, learn to face and transform our anxieties versus blocking them off and seeking pseudo solutions such as excess and violence to "fulfill" or "empower" ourselves.

I know all this sounds pie in the sky, but it is deadly serious for me and others (such as Michael Lerner [1996] with his Politics of Meaning) who propose it.

September 11th was a rip, a gash in the national fabric of routine, civility, and stability; it was also a wake-up call. How long can we pursue our so-called national interests in the face of growing division in the world, in the face of the growing split between soulless capitalism (e.g., Enron) and the rabid fundamentalism (e.g., Taliban) that is its logical consequence? How long can human engagement—on both social and individual levels—be squelched?

And yet as September 11th amply demonstrated, and as the debacle in Ukraine amplifies today, if we do not cultivate this engagement, this temper of carnival, then in the long run we may not be able to sustain a civilization at all, let alone concern ourselves with peace. Perhaps, just perhaps, this is again a time wherein people will reassess. But perhaps not, as people have yet to be "awe-wakened" on a massive-enough scale.

Precisely how we can bring more of the spirit of awe and carnival into our lives is very difficult to speculate. But what I can say, and do believe, is that it will have something to do with more freedom for that spirit. It will have something to do with more time for reflection, for engagement with family, and for recreation. It will have something to do with the creation of new ritual and communal festivals that celebrate life's wonder. It will have something to do with increased opportunities to innovate on the jobsite (as appropriate), and it will have something to do with increased participation in the meaning and implications of one's job for the community around one. It will also have to do with increased exchanges among cultures and the opportunity to explore diverse lifestyles. Finally, it will have something to do with the poetry of transgression, as suggested earlier, with providing socially sensitive outlets for people to live a little dangerously, a little perversely, and a little unpredictably (Rank, 1989). This is the secret of tragic art, and of the monster tale that so many of us in professional and political circles so readily overlook.

Afterword

It is worth noting that Franz Fanon (2004), who is being read with increased interest today, also spoke to the issue of excess as a necessary counterweight to oppressive circumstances such as the psychological and physical colonization of his day (and ours if we are to be candid). Fanon also saw aspects of excess, and even violence, as potentially enlivening and liberating for the party that is victimized by such oppressive circumstances. In this sense, his work—and that of Sartre in his introduction to Fanon's classic *The Wretched of the Earth*—is relevant to the thesis I put forth in the foregoing chapter. Yet it is also of note that Fanon (2004) expressed some discomfort with the violence in himself and others as a reaction to the oppression they encountered; therefore, in my view, this discomfort pointed to the need for awe-based reflection and deliberativeness as distinct from purely fear-driven reflex as integral to one's motivation for excess. My sense is that Fanon would also agree with the position that one's cause (whether revolution or reform) would be markedly more beneficial to people if it drew notably from awe-based reflection and deliberativeness—love of life—rather than merely fear-based reactivity. That being said, I realize that there may be a variety of interpretations of Fanon's view, and that mine is but one that may be of value to consider. I do not at all hold myself out as an expert on, or even complete sympathizer with, Fanon's perspective.

Chapter 8

Finding Life-Enhancing Anxiety During a Plague: What Existentialists Can Teach Us About COVID-19[1]

Existential thinkers have a long history of poignant responses to crises, and a sampling of these may be of help to us now. When the capacity to respond outwardly is limited, as in the case of COVID-19, existentialists have taught us much about responding inwardly. Specifically, they have taught us that when it comes to the great problems of life, imagination and intuition—or, in short, *attitude*—is an immeasurable asset.

In the winter of 1974, cultural anthropologist and Pulitzer Prize winning author Ernest Becker lay dying in a Canadian hospital. At the tender age of 49, Becker had just completed his masterwork, *The Denial of Death.* and agreed to meet with Sam Keen of *Psychology Today* magazine for what was to be his final public statement. After several rich interchanges, Keen then posed the clincher: "You have thought harder and more about death...than most anybody in the modern world and [now] I would like to ask you what you can add as a person."

Becker paused a moment, gathered his thoughts, and replied with one of the most spellbinding death-bed reflections I have ever heard:

> The most important thing to know [is] that beyond the absurdity of one's life, beyond the apparent injustice of things, beyond the human viewpoint... there is the fact of the tremendous creative energies of the cosmos which are using us for some purposes we don't know and to be used for divine purposes, however we may be misused... is the thing that I think consoles. (Becker, 1974, p. 78)

---

[1] Author's Note: This chapter is slightly adapted from a blog in *Psychology Today* Online. Copyright Sussex Publishers, LLC.

The inner freedom to respond to, rather than passively collapse before, tragedy was also a hallmark of the philosophy of existential psychiatrist Viktor Frankl. Frankl's ordeal at Auschwitz, the notorious Nazi death camp, is powerfully described in his seminal book *Man's Search for Meaning*. In this work, Frankl (1992) elaborates the most dehumanizing circumstances imaginable—daily mass executions, pervasive excrement and disease, harrowing terror and despair. But, like Becker, Frankl finds an inner resolve, a wider vision, and a notable capacity to choose his responses to calamity rather than enabling calamity to dictate its terms to him. Hence, we witness Frankl, virtually overcome, "imagining" his wife. He "hears" her answer him, "[sees] her smile," and notices "her frank and encouraging look. Real or not," he concludes, "her look was...more luminous than the sun which was beginning to rise" (p. 48).

There are many other examples of such uplift in the existential literature, and they accentuate our freedom to respond. For example, the existential poet and activist Maya Angelou, who was raped at seven years old, found her initial healing in the local library. Instead of fruitlessly self-destructing or consigning her life to bitterness, she creatively looked to literature to console her decimated spirit. There she found works by authors such as Langston Hughes and Shakespeare, that enlarged her vision, fired her imagination, and revived her dignity. The psychologist and philosopher Rollo May also tapped into his inner resources when laboring with tuberculosis in the early 1940s. Instead of capsizing in despair, which he was on the brink of doing, he found support in the work of another existential luminary, Søren Kierkegaard. Kierkegaard wrote profoundly about despair—as well as anxiety—and what he had to say inspired a profound shift in May. It pointed May, as it did the others previously discussed, to his inner choices—his approach to his calamity—rather than vain efforts to deny or eradicate it. These inner choices led to fresh ways to experience his life, such as the pursuit of a degree in psychology, a career in writing, and quite probably the improvement of his overall health.

Yet for discovering hope in the midst of despair there is probably no timelier exemplar than Albert Camus. In the closing pages of his 1948 masterwork, *The Plague*, (now on bestseller lists worldwide), Camus shows us just how significant, and indeed essential, even glimpses of inner freedom can be. Here is his insightful narrator, Dr. Rieux, commenting:

Among the heaps of corpses, the clanging bells of ambulances, the warnings of what goes by the name of fate, among unstinting waves of fear and agonized revolt, the horror that such things could be, always a great voice had been ringing in the ears of these forlorn, panicked people, a voice calling them back to the land of their desire, a homeland. It lay outside the walls of the stifled town, in the fragrant brushwood of the hills, free skies, and in the custody of love. (Camus, 1991, p. 299)

While many of us may not share the inner freedom or eloquence of the great existentialists, we can, to the extent possible, apply their chief teachings. Among these are first, recognize your ability to define rather than be defined by the circumstances that beset you; second, draw on your inner life—your memories, your imagination, your thoughts, and your feelings—to broaden your capacity to respond to rather than merely react against adversity; and, three, connect with that which you love, for there is almost always something or somebody to remind us of life's awesomeness, even in the most trying hours.

Part 3

Life-Enhancing Anxiety in Psychology

Overview

This section features two chapters that address a gap in contemporary psychology—the neglect of existentially informed, holistic perspectives in psychotherapy and positive psychology—or the psychology of "happiness." The value of life-enhancing anxiety is highlighted by greater attention to in-depth, intimate experience, as distinct from aggregated or objective reports about experience.

Chapter 9

The Case for Existential Therapy[1]

Most of our troubles as human beings are traceable to one overriding problem: our suspension in the groundlessness of existence. When a loved one dies, or we are attacked, or we fall ill, it often feels like the bottom has dropped out and there is nothing left to hold us up. Like the astronaut who's cut from her tether or the tightrope walker who slips, we suddenly come face to face, not just with our particular difficulty but with the difficulty of existence itself.

This "difficulty" is eloquently portrayed in the opening credits of the award-winning television series "Mad Men." In that signature scene, a male character is depicted in a free fall. We know very little about this character except that he is powerless, and that is revealing enough.

Trauma is a lot like this free fall. It makes us aware of what most of us, most of the day, contrive to deny: that we're all in suspense. Right now, for example, you're probably sitting on a comfortable chair in a building that feels solidly anchored to the ground, but this is not at all the complete picture. What is more fully taking place is that you're sitting on a comfortable chair in a building that rests on a gigantic ball that is whirling around the sun at 67, 000 miles per hour. This ball, furthermore, is situated in a galaxy that's hurtling through the universe at 1.2 million miles an hour to a destination that is completely unknown. And as if that is not enough, you don't really know where you came from to get to this chair and building. Oh, I know you'll probably tell me that you made a thousand arrangements to arrive at this particular place and time and that you can trace them all back to your past. But this doesn't really tell me much; nor does the ostensibly brilliant presumption that well before you arranged anything you were the "happy" product of a stray sperm and a receptive egg. The fact is that so much of what we take for granted, even today, is a culturally sanctioned artifact, a stop-gap set against a sea of bewilderment.

---

[1] Author's Note: This chapter is slightly adapted from a blog *at Psychology Today* Online. Copyright Sussex Publishers, LLC

Trauma, which literally means shock, has a way of stripping bare this culturally sanctioned frame. It has a way of rupturing our culturally agreed upon security systems—for example, our bodies, our jobs, and our identities—and exposing us to our noncontrollable roots. And what happens when we come face to face with these roots? Depending on our own traumatic histories, this encounter tends to jar us in either of two directions: toward expansive grandiosity to overcompensate for the fragility we feel, or toward constrictive withdrawal to overcompensate for the unsustainability of grandiose expansion. Yet either way we are imprisoned by these extremes, and both sabotage our growth.

The idea here then is not so much to "get rid of" a condition that's inherently human but to help people to develop a new relationship to that condition. Helping people develop a new relationship to a shocking part of themselves is not easy, but this is precisely what existentially oriented therapy attempts to promote. It attempts to help people face and gradually realign themselves with the groundlessness of their existence. What does such realignment look like? It looks like an improved ability to experience choice within that groundlessness; and to engage one's capacity to respond to rather simply react against its ferocity.

The chief and ongoing question of an existentially oriented therapy is: How is one willing to live, in this remarkable moment, with this exceptional opportunity to encounter one's pain? As my client, Janice,[2] sat across from me one Friday afternoon, I tried my best to appreciate the struggle she experienced, and the awkwardness with which she attempted to convey it. It was the first time Janice and I met, and from the moment we shook hands I could sense a cloud over her demeanor.

Janice was a 45-year-old white working-class female with a history of severe emotional and sexual abuse. Her father was an inveterate alcoholic with an explosive temper, and her grandfather sexually molested her when she was eight years old. When Janice was four, she would be regularly left alone with a "schizophrenic" aunt. These visits terrified Janice, but apparently there was no parental recognition of this sentiment. When Janice was five, her mother suddenly died. This left Janice with her volatile alcoholic father, her rapacious grandfather, and her psychotic aunt. How Janice even partially emerged from these circumstances is still a mystery to me, but somehow she managed.

---

[2] Note: The case of Janice is a composite drawn from my practice and not reflective of any individual client.

As Janice and I greeted each other, I was struck by her composure and bright, articulate style. Janice told me that although she had brief brushes with therapy in her past, she did "tons" of work on her own. I emphatically believed that. Although Janice ostensibly came to therapy because of her lack of assertiveness with men, I sensed—and in her tacit way she conveyed—that the assertiveness issue was not her ultimate concern.

At first, I worked with Janice to help her build confidence when she confronted men. I invited her to engage in role plays with me where I would stand in for the menacing fellow (e.g., her boss or husband), and she would play herself in a particular dilemma. I also worked with Janice to cognitively restructure her thinking about how these men perceived her. Would she really be seen as a "bitch" if she clarified her needs to them, I would ask. And even if she was seen that way, would that make her one? As we deepened and rehearsed these scenarios, Janice was gradually able to develop new skills that would help her confront and successfully assert herself with the aforementioned men.

At the same time as she worked with these cognitive and behavioral restructuring skills, however, something else began to happen to Janice: She began to acknowledge, and I encouraged her to stay present to, fears that went beyond feeling intimidated by men. These fears related to a sense of being intimidated by life. In this context, she began to share powerful dreams with me, like a dream she had recently of feeling like a burned-out tree, and another about a monster attacking her home. In time I took the risk to invite Janice not just to "talk about" such dreams and fantasies but to experience them here and now with me. I invited her, in other words, to become more present to how she felt, sensed, and pictured these dreams and fantasies. I also invited her to share her responses about what it was like to interact with me and to experience the difficult sides of herself, like shame or weakness, in my presence. This brought the work alive between me and Janice and significantly deepened our bond. It also enabled Janice to plumb depths only hinted at during our cognitive restructuring exercises. Finally, it moved Janice to realize how her suffering stemmed not just from her relationships with men (and sometimes women) but to her relationship with life's uncertainties and to the need for courage in the face of them.

In this vein, Janice began to allude to a whole new language in our work together—a language that emphasized her concerns about existence, not just specific aspects of existence. For example, she started speaking about "unnamable fears" and a part of herself that felt like a "black hole." She told me she had never acknowledged these feelings with anyone before, but that she had often glimpsed them, especially when stressed. She also began talking about wonderments that she had rarely ever disclosed, such as her fascination with the occult and her resonance with ancient Mayan culture. When I shared my puzzlement about these identifications, given her background, she quipped: "They are freeing, and in tune with the natural world."

In my experience, these ranges of resonance are not all that extraordinary in depth existential therapy. As people feel safer to explore, they begin to unveil the parts of themselves that both torment and, potentially, set them free. These parts are not necessarily Freudian in nature. They don't necessarily evoke sexual or aggressive conflict or frustrated parental attachments. But they do, in my experience, stir very primordial undercurrents, some of which pertain directly to sexual, aggressive, or attachment conflicts. To put it succinctly, these undercurrents strike me and others who witness them as emphatically existential in nature, pertaining not just to turbulent sexually aggressive drives or attachments to parental figures but fears and desires toward the uncontrollability of existence itself. For example, behind the fear (and sometimes attraction) of aggression can be an even deeper anxiety about imminent disarray, uncontrollability, and ultimately chaos. Or beneath the terror of parental devaluation can be the thornier challenge of one's significance in existence.

These were precisely the mooring points I faced with Janice on a fateful afternoon some six months following our initial meeting. Janice was on the brink of a breakthrough, and we both knew it. But she also grappled with great fears and the need to come to terms with those fears. On this basis, I invited Janice to simply close her eyes and become aware of her breathing. As she seemed ready, I then invited her to become aware of any tension areas she experienced in her body, any areas that felt tight or blocked that she was willing to describe. She began by identifying a tension in her neck area, which loosened as she stayed present to it. Then she began perceiving an image of a tiny girl trapped in a well. She couldn't identify where this well was or how it got there, but she was clear that it felt fathomless, with no end in sight. As I continued to invite her to stay present to this well, she began to feel the girl's terror. "It's like she's sinking," Janice told me, "and she doesn't know where she's going." Gently I supported her to continue with the experience, while at the same time reassuring her that if she needed to stop, she could do so at any time. She chose to proceed.

At about halfway into our session, Janice noticed that the little girl was fading, while the darkness around her grew. At times, the little girl struggled to unfold herself and peek out of the darkness, but invariably she sank back in. At this point Janice had said very little about her relationship to the little girl, but as she "stayed with" her, her sense of connection grew. Suddenly, Janice panicked. She could no longer find the little girl!

Yet a moment later, tears welled up in Janice's eyes. I asked her what brought on the tears and after a long silence she whispered: "I reached out into the dark to touch her, and she reached out into the dark to touch me."

With this simple yet profound image, Janice began a remarkable self-transformation. She moved from a position of abject terror to one of wonder to one of love. Through embracing the little girl, Janice at the same time embraced the void in which the little girl (as well as adult Janice) had languished for many years; and now she found solace there, as well as a chance for self-renewal.

I won't say that this moment completely changed Janice's life, but it went a long way toward freeing her and relieving her panic. Although the specifics of Janice's life—for example, her long-time employment and her involvement with her family—essentially remained the same, what she brought to those specifics altered dramatically. She now had an expanded capacity to feel, for example, a deepened experience of the moment, and a broader appreciation of life's possibilities. In the end, Janice learned much more than assertiveness skills or an ability to think more "rationally": She discovered how to be present to her life, and this presence enabled her to more fully experience her life.

Coda

Psychologists today can talk until they're blue in the face about pat formulas and programmatic treatments. They can cite chemical imbalances in the brain, for example, or the lack of ability to regulate emotions, or the irrationality of conditioned thoughts as the bases for our disorders. However, until psychologists get down to the fundamental problem that fuels all these secondary conditions—our precariousness as creatures—they will be operating at a very restrictive level. The work I did with Janice had elements of this very restrictive level, and that was important work to accomplish. However, there are questions that need to be continually raised: Is helping a person to change behavior patterns and recondition thoughts enough? Or do we owe it to that person to make available a deeper dimension of self-exploration? Do we owe it to that person to enable discovery of what really matters about his or her life, wherever that may lead? I believe Janis would answer in the affirmative to these questions, as would I and many others I've known throughout my 30-year clinical career. In a review of my book *Existential-Integrative Psychotherapy*, leading psychotherapy researcher Bruce Wampold (2008) offered a bold conjecture. "It could be," he wrote "that an understanding of the principles of existential therapy is needed by all therapists, as it adds a perspective that might...form the basis for all effective treatments" (p. 6). Isn't it time that we took such propositions seriously? Or must we continue to sacrifice depth for expedience in psychotherapy, the transformed life for the alteration of routine?

Chapter 10

The Case for a Humanistic Positive Psychology[1]

I propose that despite the nay-saying, positive psychology is justifiably a branch of humanistic psychology, and that a humanistic–positive psychology would be salutary to the profession of psychology. From the standpoint of theory, I show how positive psychology shares humanistic psychology's concern with what it means to be fully, experientially human, and how that understanding illuminates the vital or fulfilled life.

However, I also show how the findings of positive psychology, particularly in the area "happiness" research, or what has recently been termed "human flourishing," stop short of the fuller aforementioned aims. Specifically, I show how positive psychology appears to oversimplify both the experience of human flourishing and its social-adaptive value.

While the positive psychology findings on flourishing are useful in limited contexts—for example, in terms of their implications for the attainment of pleasure, physical health, and cultural competency—they are inadequate with respect to the more complicated contexts of creativity, emotional depth, and social consciousness. I will detail the nature of these discrepancies, such as their implications for perception of reality, psychological growth, and capacity for self-reflection, and consider their role in an expanded vision of human resiliency.

One final note: While I wrote this article in 2011, I include it here because despite some valiant attempts (e.g., see Wong, 2012), it doesn't strike me that the scene in mainstream positive psychology—nor general psychology—has changed all that much. There is still an emphasis on "mechanistic–cognitive" perspectives that do not, in my view, provide a holistic and more accurate view of human vitality—nor

---

[1] This chapter, with slight modifications, was presented at the American Psychological Association Convention in summer 2006. It was also published under the title "Toward a Humanistic Positive Psychology: Why Can't we Just Get Along?" in The Society for Existential Analysis journal, *Existential Analysis*, Vol. 22, No. 1, 32–38, January 2011.

depravity (e.g., see FeldmanHall & van Baar, 2022; Schneider, 2022; Waterman, 2013); and there is still the problem of "happiness" correlating with giddy embraces of authoritarian leaders (Lee, 2019).

Overview

Positive psychology is justifiably a branch of humanistic psychology. Let me clarify: To the extent that humanistic psychology stands for "What it means to be fully and experientially human, and how that understanding illuminates the vital and fulfilled life"—and it does, according to humanistic texts (e.g., see Moss, 2015; Schneider, Pierson, & Bugental, 2015, p. xvii)—I hereby advocate for a branch of humanistic psychology called positive psychology.

I am happy (and I use that word advisedly!) to endorse humanistic psychology as a positive psychology, and positive psychology as a humanism—with one major caveat: Positive psychology, as it is presently constituted, reflects what I call a "narrow band," cognitive-behaviorally informed theoretical perspective. What I mean is that prevailing studies of happiness (or even that which has been termed human flourishing) represent but a circumscribed range of how such sensibilities are actually experienced "on the ground," so to speak, in people's everyday worlds. If this were not the case, I don't think we'd see so many contradictory cases in positive psychology research, but I will elaborate on this momentarily.

Broad Band vs. Narrow Band

To the extent that positive psychology is viewed for what it is—a narrow-band formulation of a broad-band experience—I welcome it into the humanistic mosaic. On the other hand, to the extent that positive psychology—that is, narrow-band investigation—is mistaken for broad-band comprehension, I have grave concerns, not just for the alliance of positive psychology and humanism, but for the alliance of our field with life.

To restate my case, I have nothing against narrow bands; within their proper contexts, they can have great value, such as their contribution to clarity, contentment, and order. The problem is that those things represent only *slices* of life, not life itself. Or to quote another wary observer of the human scene: "Twice two makes four is...not life, gentlemen, [but] the beginning of death" (Dostoyevsky, cited in Kaufmann, 1975, p. 77). Hence, while narrow bands can have great value, they can also pose great hazards, and these hazards are necessary to point out, especially today, when twice two makes four is increasingly trumpeted as constituting life.

Problems with Narrow-Band Positive Psychology

As I view it, there are three main problems with a humanistically deprived (cognitive-behaviorally informed) positive psychology: 1) methodological narrowness, 2) neglect of the tragic dimension, and 3) susceptibility to the expedient. All three bode dubiously for our society.

The positive notions of happiness and flourishing, therefore, are not just remote academic inquiries; they are innermost challenges to our nature and world today—and that is why this discussion is so imperative. Without further ado then, let me illustrate how I believe a humanistically deprived positive psychology is impacting us today, and what, if any, steps we can take to remedy this situation—that is, to reconnect humanism and positive psychology for the enhancement of psychology as a whole.

In their 2005 article in the *American Psychologist*, Fredrickson and Losada conclude that human flourishing, which they define as an "optimal range of... functioning...that connotes goodness, generativity, growth, and resilience," is predictable based on one key factor: a "positivity ratio." What is a positivity ratio? It is a quantitative proportion of positive (i.e., pleasant, grateful, upbeat, appreciative, and enjoyable) feelings over negative (i.e., unpleasant contemptuous, irritable, disdainful, and aversive) feelings (p. 678). Further, they identify a positivity ratio of 2.9 as the threshold for flourishing based on their review of the relevant research. In other words, one must attain a ratio of about three "good thoughts" to every single bad thought in order to achieve what the authors call human flourishing. Or to put it another way, the "flourishing factors of goodness ("indexed by happiness, satisfaction, and superior functioning"), generativity ("indexed by broadened thought–action repertoires and behavioral flexibility"), growth ("indexed by gains in enduring personal and social resources"), and resilience ("indexed by survival and growth in the aftermath of adversity") are significantly "linked to a positivity ratio at or above 2.9" (p. 685).

These findings are notable and help us to understand something about "optimal" human functioning within a context of narrowly operationalized definitions, strictly codified measures, and carefully controlled observations. Granted, the researchers did use what they term "nonlinear, dynamic" equations (p. 680) to account for the relative variability of emotional processing, but, nevertheless, their findings strike me as neither fluid nor dynamic (see also Friedman & Brown, 2018).

Contradictions in the Positive Findings

Furthermore, what the researchers don't help us to understand—and what will be essential to understand if we are ever to substantively broach human vitality—is how positivity ratios also appear to correlate with destructive human tendencies. For example, a growing body of research appears to suggest that what the researchers call high positivity—a disposition to pleasant, grateful, and upbeat feelings—is also associated with a dimension called "positive illusion" (relative inaccuracy regarding reality); and that negativity (or what is generally characterized as mild to moderate depression) is correlated with relatively greater accuracy concerning reality (Alloy & Abramson, 1988; Tedeschi & Calhoon, 1995). These findings, moreover, also appear to square with recent correlations between highly positive people and suppressed psychological growth, inability to self-reflect, and racial intolerance (Bodenhausen, Kramer & Susser, 1994; Stambor, 2005, p. 13).

Furthermore, if we couple the above findings on positivity with the consistent findings that approximately 80% of the American (U.S.) population calls itself happy (*Time* Magazine, January 2005), then we have some very puzzling (some would say troubling) juxtapositions to account for. For example, a quarter of the U.S. population (presumably a healthy percentage of the happy 80%) believes that "using violence to get what they want is acceptable" (Rifkin, 2005, p. 32). Nearly half "are more likely to believe that human nature is basically evil, and that 'one must belong to the one true religion to lead the best, most meaningful life'" (*Spirituality & Health*, May/June, 2005, p. 27); 59% believe that the prophesies in the Book of Revelation (such as the rapture and a war with Islam in the final reckoning) are going to come true; and nearly a quarter believe that the Bible predicted the 9/11 attacks (Moyers, 2005). And if we are to surmise that happiness is an indicator of physical well being, how do we account for the findings that 67% of U.S. men and 57% of U.S. women are overweight or obese (Payne, 2005)?

Even more troubling, the researchers fail to explain how high positivity seems to be linked with some of the most egregious forms of behavior in the history of our world, to wit: the eye-witness reports of

Nazi party rallies, Stalinist marches, Klan gatherings etc., and the mass enthrallment with authoritarian leaders (Shirer, 1960; Goldhagen, 1996). Seasoned journalist William Shirer, for example, noted that by the time of his Nuremberg address in the early 1930s, Hitler had received "the most frenzied adulation for a public figure that [he had] ever seen" (p. 230).

On a much tamer level, although still to the point, Richard Handler (2006), a reporter for the *Psychotherapy Networker* wrote at the conclusion of a positive psychology course taught by no less than its acclaimed founder that:

> Seligman has undoubtedly done the field of psychology an enormous service by demonstrating that...the study of what makes people happy, optimistic, and wise is just as important as the study of what makes them anxious, depressed, and crazy....And yet I am still left wondering if...the will to try for the optimistic life must come from something deeper, more mysterious, [and] less definable. (p.12)

Oddly enough, "Handler concluded, "while we were never supposed to give in to negativity and depression, they both shadowed the whole course; they were the unacknowledged elephants lurking in the corner" (p. 11).

Perhaps genuine happiness is not something you aim at, but is, as Frankl once noted, a byproduct of a life well lived, and a life well lived does not settle on the programmed or neatly calibrated. Consider Rollo May's (1981, pp. 241–242) distinction between happiness and the more rewarding (in his view) "joy:"

> Happiness depends generally on one's outer state; joy is an overflowing of inner energies and leads to awe and wonderment....Happiness is the absence of discord; joy is the welcoming of discord as the basis of higher harmonies. Happiness is finding a system of rules which solve our problems; joy is taking the risk that is necessary to break new frontiers. (pp. 241–242)

Summary and Conclusion

In short, positive psychology and its cognitive-behaviorally informed theoretical base have a lot of explaining to do. If scoring high on positive psychology scales—which often means enjoying lots of friends and family and frequently going to church—encompasses the oblivious couch potato as well as the fanatical ideologue, something is amiss.

Furthermore, the ratio of positive to negative feelings would seem to be a very crude indicator indeed of the highly nuanced and multimodal experiences of flourishing and happiness. On the other hand, a humanistically informed positive psychology, in my view, could help redress that explanatory chasm. By marshalling perceptive, subtly nuanced, quantitative *and* qualitative data, we may discover a very different portrait of the "flourishing" person. This portrait would likely unveil a many-textured personality—closer to Zorba the Greek[2] than to Dick or Jane—who may well keep a clean and orderly life but who, at the same time, may also quietly endorse a materialist, militarist, and imperialist lifestyle. How else will we find out about such discrepancies unless we employ methodologies that cut beneath the deceptive surfaces of human performance (Shedler, Mayman, & Manis, 1993).

Hence, in answer to the question that I posed at the beginning of this chapter about what it means to be fully, experientially human and how that illuminates the vital life, I advocate for a humanistically informed positive psychology, one that would supplement positive psychology's scales with in-depth portraitures and augment positive psychology's theorizing with theorizing that accounts for the ranges of human fulfillment.

In his study of self-actualizers, Abe Maslow (1968) made a similar point. He said that these most mature people were also very childlike, and that despite their exceedingly strong egos, they could be "most egoless, self-transcending, and problem-centered" (p. 140).

"Now it is very curious," wrote Rollo May (1995, p. 99), along a parallel line of investigation, "that each of [the creative therapists May admired] was great in exactly his weakest point." For example, "Harry Stack Sullivan, the person who could never relate to others, founded...interpersonal [psychiatry];" Abe Maslow, "who had so many hellish experiences [as a child growing up in the streets of New York] founded...the school of peak experience and the human potential movement." May goes on: "The experience of degeneration...is I hope, temporary, but [it] can often be used as a way of reforming and

---

[2] Greek psychologists have a wonderful term that draws in part from Kazantzakis's classic *Zorba the Greek*: It is called "Oistros" and it literally means a "love of life" (see Georganda, 2020).

reorganizing ourselves on a higher level. As C.G. Jung puts it, 'the gods return in our diseases'" (p.100).

And it is precisely for reasons like these that we need a humanistically informed positive psychology. Far from being diversionary—or, God forbid, fuzzy-minded(!)—a humanistically informed positive psychology would aim straight at the paradoxes of human flourishing, resolutely excavating its depths, complexities, and ambiguities (Schneider, 2004, 2009). A humanistically informed positive psychology would acknowledge the capacities of depression or anger or fear to distort, but it would also, and at the same time, recognize their capacities to clarify, liberate, and sensitize. In short, a humanistically informed positive psychology would foster a brute inquiry of being. Such an inquiry would be forged in "the lived truth of the terror of creation," as the noted anthropologist, Ernest Becker (1973, p. 283) once phrased it, "with full exercise of passion, of vision, of pain, of fear, and of sorrow" (p. 84). Anything less, as he also noted, would be a dereliction of both our science and our humanity.

Part 4

Social and Political Applications of Life-Enhancing Anxiety

Overview

This section elaborates social and political applications of life-enhancing anxiety through three lenses. The first lens is that which I call the "fluid center," which is an "awe-based" consciousness exemplified by "the richest possible range of experience within the most suitable parameters of support." It can also be understood as "playful constraint, humble daring, and reverent adventurousness." The second lens is a highly structured and supportive conflict mediation model I call the "Experiential Democracy Dialogue." The Experiential Democracy Dialogue is a one-on-one format that supports individuals from highly contrasting (cultural and political) backgrounds to experience one another more as human beings rather than stereotypes or labels, and through that process enhance the likelihood of achieving common ground. Finally, the third lens in this section calls for a mass mobilization of what I term "emotionally restorative relationships" in our country and, by implication, the world. Emotionally restorative relationships help people to feel seen and heard and get at the roots of their problems. In my view, we have an alarming dearth of such relationships at home and abroad right now; and if we don't address the situation urgently, we risk inexorable long-term collapse.

Chapter 11

The Fluid Center:
An Awe-Based Challenge to Society[1]

This chapter raises two basic questions: What is existential–humanistic psychology's relevance to post 9/11/2001? and Can that relevance be practically applied to daily life? To address these questions, I elaborate on a concept that I call the "fluid center." The fluid center is an "awe-based" consciousness exemplified by playful constraint, humble daring, and reverent adventurousness. Whereas 9/11 represented the triumph of personal and interpersonal polarization (e.g., arrogance, humiliation), the fluid center, by contrast, represents the opportunity for personal and interpersonal revitalization (e.g., discerning openness, mindful dialogue). To illustrate this position, I propose two social visions that draw on the fluid center: awe-based education and awe-based vocation. I conclude that not only can such alternatives modify institutional settings; they can radically transform lives.

Introduction

The blow to American prestige, innocence, and conviction on September 11th, 2001, raises key questions for humanistic psychology and the humanistic movement. If some people were skeptical of humanistic psychology's social and global relevance before September 11th, they may now have cause to be dismissive. How, for example, can the time-honored humanistic qualities of warmth, empathy, and genuineness, reach suicide bombers, dispossessed refugees, and starving children? What do sincere invitations to dialogue mean to

---

[1] Author's Note: This chapter was adapted from an article titled "The Fluid Center: A Third Millennium Challenge to Culture" in *The Humanistic Psychologist, 27* (1), 114-130. Copyright 1999 by the American Psychological Association. Portions of the chapter are also elaborated on in my book, *Rediscovery of Awe: Splendor, Mystery, and the Fluid Center of Life* [Paragon House, 2004]).

anthrax manufacturers, enraged clerics, and resentful mobs? In the age-old clash of cultural heritages, where is the place for human potential?

These are not trivial controversies, and they will try the patience of us all. But they will especially challenge those who have supported and worked hard to implement humanistic causes. Yet I, for one, am not ready to simply discard these steadfast efforts, and certainly not for some square-jawed cynicism! On the contrary, we need to call upon the humanistic visionary tradition as never before in the coming years. And to the degree we neglect it, we neglect hope.

What is the humanistic visionary tradition? First let us dispel what it is not. It is not simply American "do goodism," or optimistic individualism, or capricious libertinism; it is not synonymous with the New Age or, as some positive psychologists are wont to assert, the appraising of crystals. It is a dynamic and evolving heritage, a supple heritage that encompasses Greek, Renaissance, and Romantic lineages. Today, these lineages intertwine with existential, transpersonal, and constructivist theorizing and converge on one overarching concern: What does it mean to be fully experientially human, and how does that understanding illuminate the vital or fulfilled life? (Schneider, Pierson, & Bugental, 2015).

In the interest of the latter, I propose that the blasting of the Pentagon and World Trade Towers echoes a wider, more insidious phenomenon: the blasting of human souls. This blasting has been taking place perennially, and it gets perennially overlooked. The blasting to which I refer is the smashing of human aspiration, the bashing of human integrity, and the stanching of human vitality. It is the stunting of human freedom, and, conversely, the accentuating of human arrogance. It is a floodtide that knows no bounds; it bleeds into the streets as well as the suites, the steel girders as well as the ivory towers.

The blasting of which I speak is an existential blasting; a blasting of revenge and of desperation, a blasting by little people who aspire to become big people, and a blasting by big people who deny that they are also little people—and on the cycle spins. As long as there is destitution, desperation, and impotence in this world, there will be vain attempts at reversal—greatness, glory, and omnipotence. As long as people are polarized, they will court further polarization. In this chapter, I want to suggest that our core polarization is between our smallness (fragility, limitedness), and our greatness (resiliency, expansiveness), and that both must be acknowledged for us to thrive (Schneider, 1990).

The repeated problem is that people cut off both of these potentialities. They become trapped, fixated, and estranged. They swing from pole to pole and miss the vibrancy between the poles. How, then, are we to redress these perennial pitfalls; what will help humanity to become whole?

Let me suggest three ways, which all lead down the same basic path by bringing awe, carnival, and what I call the fluid center more explicitly into our consciousness. By awe I mean the cultivation of the basic human capacity for the thrill and anxiety of living or, more formally, the cultivation of the capacity for humility and boldness, reverence and wonder before creation (e.g., this is the mysterium et fascinans that Rudolf Otto [1923/1958] speaks of to describe the numinous; it is the capacity to be deeply moved).

By carnival, I mean the importation of a sense of play, multi-dimensionality, and contrariety into our lives—but all within a relatively safe and structured context. The idea here is that, ironically, the more we can play with the various "parts" of ourselves, the more deeply we can come to know ourselves, the parts of ourselves that genuinely matter.

Finally, by the fluid center, I mean the cultivation of all these dimensions—elasticity, pausefulness: the richest possible range of experience within the most suitable parameters of support (or any sphere of consciousness that has as its concern the widest possible relation to existence).

These are the same ideas that I believe Nietzsche was getting at with his "passionate people who become masters of their passion" (cited in Kaufmann, 1968, p. 280); or Malinowski with his "freedom" as the "acceptance of the chains which suit" one; and Ortega with his aspirations to a "vital design" (cited in May, 1981, pp. 83 and 93). If it doesn't have paradox, if it doesn't have contradiction, the philosopher Phillip Hallie, once intimated, "it isn't a powerful human feeling" (cited in Moyers, 1988).

I want to suggest that there are two pivotal settings where American and indeed contemporary Western culture lack this sense of the paradoxical, the awesome, the carnivalesque, and the fluidly centered: school and work.

On the pages that follow, I will describe two humanistic social proposals that address the aforementioned settings. While these proposals are hypothetical and somewhat crudely drawn, they provide a crucial window, I believe, on trenchant, humanity-wide reform.

Toward an Awe-Based Educational Curriculum

In a stunningly neglected treatise, Ernest Becker (1967) sets forth an equally stunning educational proposal: the "alienation curriculum." The alienation curriculum is Becker's strategy to engage students, to animate their educational experience. In a nutshell, the curriculum teaches students how various cultures down through history have handled alienation. The curriculum inquires, in effect, how various societies have estranged (e.g., humiliated, aggrandized; polarized, fetishized) their populaces throughout history, and to what extent such practices relate to students' current lives.

While there are many welcome dimensions to this curriculum—and it would no doubt benefit students immensely—I would like to propose a broader and more affirming curriculum that I believe would have even greater salutary effects. Drawing from Becker's proposal, then, I will now set forth an idea to enhance and complement the movement toward a fluid center at work, at home, and in places of worship. This proposal is for an awe-based educational curriculum. Again, awe is defined as the capacity for the thrill and anxiety of living (the capacity to be moved); it is further defined as the realization of the humbling and emboldening sides of living, not as separate poles but together as integrated "wholes" of experience. In a nutshell, awe comprises an integrated sensibility of discovery, adventure, and boldness melded to and in the context of safety, structure, and support. Awe mitigates against alienation (polarization), either in the form of hyper-humility (humiliation) or hyper-boldness (arrogance).

How then, might we initiate an awe curriculum? I propose that we begin with a cohort of middle school students studying history. (Note that elementary school students could also be given some form of this curriculum. The issue is not so much the form of the curriculum as the infusion of the curriculum with a spirit of awe; and while this spirit does not preclude more technical kinds of training [e.g., reading, writing, arithmetic], these technologies are employed in the service of, or as an adjunct to, awe-based inquiry. It is only in later years, as students are ready to specialize, that such skills as math and science would be focused upon as separate domains).

The question to students could be: How have given cultures throughout history affirmed or suppressed a sense of awe (humility and wonder), and what does that affirmation or suppression imply for students' current lives? For example, students could study (and participate in field trips concerning) a range of historical epochs. These could span from the Neolithic, Egyptian, Hebrew, Greco–Roman, Early Christian, Medieval, Renaissance, Enlightenment–Romanticist, and industrial–technological to the non-Western (e.g., Eastern and African) contexts.

Beginning with the cultures of the Near and Middle East (e.g., Babylon, Greece, Egypt), students might then be asked to look at some sample traditions and how and whether they foster awe, as defined above. Students might be asked to consider, for example, the relationship of these cultures to land and nature; their religious systems—pantheism, goddess worship, mystery cults; their architecture—palaces, marketplaces, sacred sites; their art, literature, and philosophy; their forms of government; their transitions from agrarianism to urbanism and pantheism to monotheism. But also let us not neglect to alert students to the disease and pestilence in these societies; fatigue and overwork (where the average life span is in the 20s, the 60s if one is elite); slavery (if any), elitism, and barbarity. Let us encourage students to reflect on the societies' structure of authority—for example, collective vs. individualist, elite vs. communal—and their concept of personal autonomy.

Next, we would ask students how these awe-inspiring (humbling and emboldening) and awe-deflating (humiliating and aggrandizing) episodes relate to their present lives, their present worlds. In what ways might they adopt/draw upon these discoveries to enhance or reform their worlds? Some possible discussion questions include: What is the potential role of nature and natural environments on students' present sensibilities? What is the current significance of feminist spiritual principles (nurturance, egalitarianism)? What is the place of the sense of the sacred vs. formal religion today? What is the present role of aesthetics in architecture? What are the various forms of slavery (compulsion, addiction) in today's lifestyles? What about the contemporary forms of elitism and barbarity? What is the relevance of individual vs. collective authority, autonomy vs. community today?

Other discussion areas could include the decadence of Rome, political rebellion and the institutional church in early Christianity, chivalry and sexuality during the Middle Ages, rationality vs. religion during the Renaissance and so on.

In sum, the awe curriculum is an ideal or mooring point; it does not have to be adopted in its entirety or literally, as I have presented it. There are many small ways that teachers can begin—and, indeed, are beginning—to adopt an awe curriculum in their current repertoire of courses. Among these are: asking students about the relevance of a given subject (e.g., English literature, astronomy, social science) to their current lives, their visions of a future world, and their hopes, dreams, or visions of making an impact on that future world; introducing "awe"—the thrill and anxiety, humility and wonder of living—as a concept, and relating that concept to a given subject area (e.g., how American fiction illustrates awe and what that awe evokes in students' lives); showing how various parts of the sciences such as mathematics, life sciences, and anthropology inspire awe and what this inspiration implies for students' environmental, social, or spiritual concerns. The presentation of these ideas in plays, stories, and expressive arts could also be implemented. There are many creative avenues to explore.

Awe-Based Work Programs

The class and income disparities in the world, particularly in the United States, are grievous—as many readers are aware. This is a condition where in 1999, 19% of American children lived in poverty (the worst rate in the developed world); where in 1992, the average American executive made 419 times what the average factory worker made; and where the top 2.7% of wage earners made as much as the bottom 100 million (Intelligence Report, 1999). It's a world where a camp counselor can and often does earn more than a frontline mental health worker at a home for disturbed children (Sebastian Earl, personal communication, 1999), or an information technologist makes several times the salary of a social worker, or a professional basketball player makes 100 times the wages of a teacher.

We profess to desire an engaged and invigorated populace. We say we want an informed and unified citizenry. We advertise our yen for physically and emotionally healthy children; youth who are committed to the values of work and brotherly love. Despite the rhetoric, however, we have a very puzzling way of demonstrating our concerns. How is it, for example, that our economic system is virtually tailor made to subvert our alleged values; and how is it that our morals, relationships, and lifestyles are for all intents and purposes contrary to our pronouncements? The question is: Can conventional notions of success be converted into visionary notions, can "enrichment" mean capacity for humility, reverence, and wonder—awe—before creation?

While the first step toward such a transformation has already been suggested with an awe-based educational curriculum, presently, I will outline an awe-based work proposal. What if (indulge my fantasies for a moment!) we could pass the following legislation: All non-employer income earners in the top 2% of the American adult population and all American employers whose combined yearly individual income also exceeds the top 2% of wage earners would be offered a choice—either invest in (tax reduced) awe-based, socially responsible benefit programs or pay steep and sustained government taxes (which will in turn fulfill the same purpose)?

The socially responsible investment plan would comprise two components—a comprehensive, universal health plan and for the employed, a one-hour program in mental well-being, and a one-hour session in physical well-being weekly. The health plan would be partially subsidized by the government (from the general tax fund and the top 2% of employer and nonemployer income earners), and the well-being programs would be funded solely by the top 2% of employer income earners (or, if agreed upon in advance, by an entire company). The health plan would provide generous mental and physical health benefits determined by both federal and regional authorities.

How would we get such a program implemented? First, I believe that many people—employees in particular—would welcome such an idea (especially if clearly articulated). Second, although many employers would balk at the expenditure of such a program, they would soon realize that they are all on the same playing field and that if they want to remain in the game they have to find a way to play—and play it well. While cost-shifting (e.g., passing on expenditure costs to consumers) could be a problem, I believe that it would remain manageable because all employers in this bracket would be in the same situation and, therefore, would have to keep their prices competitive.

Finally, although there would likely be some suppression of incentive to become a top wage earner, employer, and entrepreneur in the light of our proposal, especially among more materialistic types, there are three issues that I believe would mitigate this problem: First, everyone would be in the same boat, as previously mentioned, so jealousy, extravagant expectations and the like would, by implication, be delimited. Second, people would soon find that there would still be room for healthy profit and wage earnings in spite of and perhaps even in light of the increased social consciousness at a given work-setting (e.g., because of the greater social relevance of that setting's structure and product line). And last but not least, most, if not all, prospective workers will have undergone the awe-based educational training I alluded to earlier—and would therefore be inclined to value rather than to discount a vocational analogue of the latter.

One final note by way of context, just like the awe-based educational curriculum, awe-based vocation does not have to be a "one size fits all" proposition. There are many incremental ways to implement awe-based vocation. These can include but not be exhausted by: informal social gatherings (such as might be convened during the lunch hour), in which colleagues confer with one another about the state of their jobs, their lives on the job, and the lives they affect. Workers could also agree to hire a consultant or mediator to facilitate their dialogue on these or related subjects, or to consult with management about the implications of their discussions. There might be informal arrangements for yoga, Tai Chi, or meditation classes at the jobsite; or there might be provisions for personal counseling, and/or growth experience through outreach to services in the surrounding community. Any or all of these can be "awe" informing.

That said, I will now proceed with a description of the well-being programs outlined above. While these descriptions are more formal, and in some ways more hypothetical than the partial applications just discussed, they are not, in my view, out of reach. They are a basis for system-wide reform.

Drawing from the envisioned mandate, then, the well-being programs could be administered by a committee comprising the employer, mental and physical health providers (e.g., psychologists, psychiatrists, general practice physicians, holistic health practitioners), and employees. The programs would be voluntary and scheduled at consistent times during eight-hour work days. The mental well-being program could entail a wide variety of offerings, from topics of psychological and philosophical interest to those concerning spirituality and multiculturalism. The purpose of the mental well-being programs would be to promote reflection on, and where appropriate, corrective action concerning the impact of work on employees' and employers' lives.

Although such reflection and corrective action would be confined to work issues, they could address a wide variety of concerns. For example, the program might take the form of a discussion hour in which employers and employees consider the environmental relevance of their products; it could also take the form of a reflection about the need to restore pride, craftsmanship, and innovation at the worksite; it could also entail conflict mediation seminars or forums about social values. The mental well-being programs would need to fulfill four basic criteria. They would need to be 1) independently facilitated, 2) voluntary and nondiscriminatory (e.g., protected from employer retaliation), 3) relevant to the work setting, and 4) acceptable to an employer/employee well-being committee. (For issues that fall outside these categories, other healthcare/organizational services may be needed). Finally, the well-being committee would, through one of its elected representatives, have a permanent seat on the respective company's board.

The physical well-being programs could also consist of a variety of offerings and be administered by a physical well-being committee. The committee would consist of the employer, an elected body of employees, and a physical health expert of their choice. Activities could range from workout regimens to massage and sauna to yoga and stress-reduction exercises. There could also be provisions for a variety of programs on holistic health, exercise, nutrition, and alternative medicines. The on-staff health provider would help to monitor and, if necessary, medically advise all participants.

In addition to the above programs, there could be provisions for a range of alternative activities during the mental and physical well-being hours, from nature walks to outdoor retreats and communal projects (such as consumer satisfaction surveys). Those who choose not to participate in such activities would also have a variety of options from which to choose, from relaxing and recreating to continuing work.

In order to maximize the integration of work and personal activity. four-day workweeks would be implemented. Such a nonwork period is essential for reflection, loved ones, and recreation. It also structures time for those who wish to partake in civic activities. While it is true that about 10 hours would be subtracted from the conventional workweek, the 10 hours that would replace them should be more than enough to make up for such a loss; in fact, they should form the bedrock for a revolutionary new form of living because in these 10 hours people would be encouraged to reflect deeply on their jobs, their lives, and the lives of those around them. The fruits of such engagement should be manifold—from enhancement of the work environment to humanization of the social terrain, and from improved vocational motivation to elevated social and moral sensitivity. The services resulting from such a transformation should also be markedly improved.

There should be more services that address people's core values—for example, environmentally supportive transportation programs, life-enhancing architectural arrangements, and health-affirming agricultural yields. There should be marked improvements in mental and physical health, education, and rehabilitation programs. There should be more and better medical services with a wider range of treatment alternatives (e.g., low-cost, year-long psychotherapy).

There should be pervasive improvements in recreational facilities, entertainment, and sporting events. There should be dramatically fewer overpaid executives, entertainers, and athletes, and markedly increased affordability of products and services. For example, to the extent that products become more meaningful to people, they will buy them more often, which eventually should lower prices. And to the degree that entrepreneurial wealth is returned to the system that supports it, the quality and affordability of that system should also commensurately rise.

Finally, the well-being programs open up unprecedented opportunities for specialists in human service—from psychologists to physicians, philosophers to artisans, and counselors to healers. While some may decry the ferocity of that transformation, I and many others would argue that it is just the counterweight necessitated today, as technicist models for living encroach upon the cultural landscape.

Awe-based prioritization should not eliminate the former technicist model. It should not erase the significant and hard-won gains of industrialization—controlling diseases, mass producing food, expediting information. Such a call would be sheer folly, and I don't believe many of the people urging humanistic change would seriously entertain it. However, an awe-based reform should bring a deepening, a sensitizing, and a widening of our day-to-day view. It should instill the fluidity in the inert centeredness, and the flesh, bone, and heart in the pale plurality of our culture.

From this point of view, it is essential that we maintain, as Becker (1967) echoing Robert Maynard Hutchins put it, The Great Conversation—and not just in the ivory tower but in the streets and suites as well. The well-being proposal releases unprecedented creative energies for individual and social expression but—and this is key—within the existing structures of a disciplined and committed workforce. The range of possibilities arising from the well-being forums will be rich for not only will various companies opt for diverse presentations, but various Great Conversations within those presentations will impact company policymaking. Put another way, The Great Conversation should lead to a continually evolving network of ideas, expressions, and sensibilities, which should result, in turn, in an ever-growing sphere of personal and vocational enhancement. Just imagine a fellow returning home from work after an exhilarating discussion about the moral import of his product line that could impact thousands of unknowing customers, not to mention the integrity of the salesman himself. Think how this state would affect his relationship with his wife, his children, his general health, and his sense of life.

The convergence of an awe-based, meaning-based, and reflection-based pause in the middle of peoples' workday, complemented by a parallel developmental and educational experience, should have pervasive and synergistic effects on the entire ways we perceive, engage, and live out our respective days.

Postscript

Amid the talk of security, "smoking them out," and shopping as viable responses to the 9/11 tragedy, the question looms: What will be America's long-term reply to those it has enraged?

In this chapter, I have presented two potential answers to this conundrum: awe-based education and awe-based vocation. If we are to have a chance at global solidarity, then we will need a palpable change in our relations to both people and capital. We will need to complement such relations with a new set of conditions, among them the routine availability of interpersonal exchange—the sharing of joys and sorrows, hopes and estrangements—and not just in homes or barrooms but in offices and classrooms, embassies and legislatures. We will need to model what social experiments have already demonstrated—that when people can assemble together, share experiences, and learn about each other's intimate lives, they can become more tolerant of one another and more appreciative of one another's humanity (e.g., see Rogers, 1986; Bar-On, 1993; Montuori & Purser, 2015; Schneider, 2003, 2004).

Is there a more urgent time for America to provide such models, or for humanists to propose them? I echo this question again today, in 2022.

Chapter 12

Applying Life-Enhancing Anxiety to Bridge Cultural and Political Divides: The Experiential Democracy Dialogue

For the past nineteen years, I have been cultivating a dialogue-based application of life-enhancing anxiety. This application was inspired in the wake of the Iraq war two years after the terrorist attack on the World Trade Center. It was then updated and reinforced by the divisive election campaign of Donald Trump for president of the United States. In both of the above cases, I saw how quickly anxiety about terrorism in the first instance, and then anxiety about the breaking up of conservative values in the second instance devolved into verbal flame-throwing, isolative tribalism, and blatant violence. I also felt that existential and depth psychology had much to offer as an alternative to such partisanship, and that it was high time to apply it.

The conflict mediation approach I developed from my experience both as an existential–depth psychotherapist and a trained moderator for the grassroots citizens movement "Braver Angels" is what I call the "Experiential Democracy Dialogue" (EDD). The EDD is a one-on-one approach to conflict mediation that draws on the cultivation of concerted presence (or the deepening of engagement) to gradually integrate anxiety about the "otherness" in oneself and in the partner with whom one has a conflict. Through a series of phases, the conflicted partners are methodically invited to stay present to and thereby work with the parts of themselves and the other that evoke crude reactions, such as stereotypes, presumptions, and prejudices that can gradually transform into more deliberative, humanizing responses. In a word, the EDD process can help the partners *enlarge* their views of themselves and the other so that disagreements do not have to devolve into entrenched hatred but can evolve into co-existing differences. The difference between those two stances can mean the difference between abject devaluation and contempt and palpable empathy and potential for common ground. It is the difference between running as far away from one's anxiety as one can in the form of polarized and hostile defenses and working with one's anxiety in the form of engagement and discovery.

While this mediation approach is by no means for everyone, and it has been associated with many uncomfortable conversations, it also has yielded many gratifying and sometimes enduring encounters. Surprising friendships have been forged from dialogues such as the latter and lessening of tensions (Hawkins, 2022). Still, it is vital to recognize that for some, particularly people of color in marginalized communities, the idea of sitting with one's "oppressor" is like a battered spouse sitting with their abuser. It may simply not be fathomable until and unless there is a restorative justice process first. This process may take the form of a formal apology, monetary recompense, or something akin to the truth and reconciliation commission in South Africa. It also might take the form of activism in marches or legislative measures. There is assuredly a place for such righteous anger, and I do not in any way wish to discount it. In the long run, however, for many I frankly don't see a way around bridge-building dialogues of the type I described above. The alternative is a vicious cycle of antipathy.

Another way to frame all this is that the cultivation of presence is key to addressing the fear and insignificance, the groundlessness and helplessness, that drive the polarized mind. As intimated earlier in this volume, I define the polarized mind as the fixation on single points of view to the utter exclusion of competing points of view, and it is arguably responsible for more human destructiveness than any other psychosocial factor. Through the provision of presence, the EDD is one way to provide the "holding environment," as Winnicott (1965) has elaborated, and "transmuting internalization," as Kohut (1977) has proposed, that can transform the polarized mind. Formally, I define presence as the holding and illuminating of that which is palpably significant within oneself and between oneself and another.

As we will see momentarily, the EDD provides tools for cultivating presence (such as ground rules and structure) whereby utter lostness and the fear of insignificance before the "other" begins to diminish, and safety, acceptance, and curiosity begin to take their place. Note that this is an internal as well as external transformative process. The more that dialogue partners can be present to and accepting of the range of reactions within themselves, the more they are able to deal with and transcend the range of reactions they have toward the other (their partner). This process of co-presence enables dialogue partners to see the "more" both in themselves and the other. It also enables partners to see the humanity in each other, to disconfirm old stereotypes about each other, and to find possible avenues of commonality.

All that said, the dialogue process is also a palpable risk; it can and does sometimes lead to greater alienation both from oneself and one's partner, and to confirmation rather than dispelling of presumptions. The EDD, as with all substantive encounters between people, is a very multi-faceted experience that can evoke strikingly primal processes. As suggested earlier, these processes have their roots in early childhood and very likely at the point of birth itself and, thus, require a sensitivity and seriousness that not everyone is prepared to adopt. However, such extremes of negativity are not a usual byproduct of the EDD in my experience, and there are abiding alternatives (such as redirection to the ground rules or simple withdrawal) for people to address such difficulties (Schneider, 2020). Again, the aim of these conversations is not to change others' minds but to learn about and understand the other. This way of relating can and often does enhance the likelihood of achieving common ground between people, or at the least a level of valuing that delimits hostility and violence.

Several studies back the above claim. For example, the grassroots movement Braver Angels, which brings self-identified liberals and conservatives together for "living room" conversations, and which has informed the Experiential Democracy Dialogue, conducted a post-workshop survey with nearly 6,000 participants (Hawkins, 2022). The researchers found that 82% of post-workshop participants felt more connected to and less estranged from those on the other side and 86% of the participants said they understood the other side better. Moreover, 80% said they were better able to "counteract their inner polarizer and express criticism of the other side without increasing polarization," and over 77% of the participants said they were more likely to share what they learned with others following the workshops.

On a related note, the research group More in Common (2019) found that those on the liberal left and those on the conservative right were not as far apart as our media and political rhetoric would suggest. Here is a sample of their findings:

- Democrats and Republicans imagine that almost twice as many people on the other side hold extreme views than really do.
- On average, Democrats and Republicans believe that 55 percent of their opponents' views are extreme, but in reality only about 30 percent are.

- Americans with more partisan views hold more exaggerated views of their opponents.
- Members of America's "exhausted majority" have a narrower perception gap than either of the "wings" (America's more politically partisan groups).
- Consumption of most forms of media, including talk radio, newspapers, social media, and local news, is associated with a wider perception gap.
- For example, people who consume news "most of the time" are almost three times as inaccurate as those who consume it "only now and then."
- Furthermore, those who post about politics on social media show a substantially larger perception gap than those who do not.
- Higher education among Democrats, but not Republicans, corresponds with a wider perception gap.
- For example, Democrats who hold a postgraduate degree are three times as inaccurate as those who did not graduate high school.
- This may be due in part to lower friendship diversity, as higher educated Democrats (but not Republicans) are more likely to say that "almost all" of their friends share their political views.
- The wider people's perception gap, the more likely they are to attribute negative personal qualities (like "hateful" or "brainwashed") to their opponents.
- Overall, Americans' views are more similar to those of their political opponents than they realize. Most Americans identify as either Democrats or Republicans, and while these sides often have very different approaches, as I have found in Braver Angels groups, they tend to share bedrock values, such as the importance of personal and interpersonal safety, freedom, and fairness.

While this research reveals disturbing trends, the overall message is not as discouraging as some may think, and person to person *dialogue* the authors conclude is key to both revealing and fruitfully drawing upon commonalities.

Finally, a recent Rand Corporation study (Brown et al., 2021) found that ex-members of extremist political and religious groups were more apt to become alienated and entrenched in their views when they felt talked down to or "taught" to change their behavior by outside groups. But when ex-members, either through self-initiation or circumstance, actually met or became exposed to people of diverse backgrounds, that was a decisive factor in their willingness to change and leave their former extremist niches.

To gain a greater understanding of the life-enhancing anxiety of Experiential Democracy Dialogues, consider the following points, summarized below, that elaborate the way the Experiential Democracy Dialogue proceeds with dyad partners. This format encompasses the ground rules, the set-up (for dyad partners to select the topic of their conversation), and dialogue phases 1–6:

Summary
The Experiential Democracy Dialogue for Two[1]

Ground Rules

- We are here to understand others and explain our views, not to convince others to change their mind.
- Let's each of us try to speak for ourselves and not try to speak for or represent any outside group.
- Let's stick to the spirit of the activities designed for each phase of the dialogue.
- Otherwise, this is standard stuff we all know: taking turns, not interrupting others, listening to others, being respectful (e.g., as in no eye-rolling, or loud sighs when someone is speaking).
- In other words, bring your best selves to a difficult conversation. Try your best to come from a place of curiosity, respect (if not for the partner's belief than at least for their willingness to engage in civil, present dialogue with you), and openness.

Dialogue Set-Up (2 Minutes)
Partners decide on topic and the liberal or conservative (or other polarized) positions they'll respectively take. Some partners may need to role play someone they know who conflicts with them. Example topics:

---

[1] Author's note: This summary is adapted from *The Depolarizing of America: A Guidebook for Social Healing* (University Professors Press, 2020). The book's credo is curiosity, respect, and openness, which enhances the prospect of achieving common ground. It is highly recommended that dialogue partners read the aforementioned book to attain the optimal background for this dialogue process.

- How do you feel society is dealing with political polarization, the pandemic, racism, economic or other crises of your choosing? (choose one issue)
- How are *you* dealing with political polarization, the pandemic, racism, economic or other crises of your choosing? (choose one issue)

Please remember to adhere to the Ground Rules

Dialogue Phases

Phase One: Visualizing the Dialogue (4 Minutes)
Each partner begins by silently visualizing what it might be like to engage in (a given) dialogue with the other partner.

- (2 mins.) Each partner is invited to observe, without fixating on, the feelings, sensations, and thoughts that come up when visualizing the dialogue with the other. (Simply acknowledge and do your best to co-exist with the tensions and differences that emerge.)
- (2 mins.) Each partner finally is invited to envision—clear a space for—the humanity of their partner, their flesh and blood humanness, vulnerability, and personal story beyond the initial "stamp" you impose on them

Phase Two: Background (10 Minutes)
Invitation for each dialogue partner to describe their background and summarize very briefly what it was like growing up *and* how their family/culture treated the ideological "other" as related to the issue at hand. (Thus, if the topic is on a political difference, talk about how that political difference, such as gun-rights or racism, was handled by caretakers. This elaborates the context for one's perspective.) [5 mins for each partner].

Phase Three: Taking a Stance (12 Minutes)
Invitation for each partner to tell, as mindfully and heartfully as possible, their "side" of an issue without interruption, followed by paraphrases of what was heard by the listener, with chance for correction.

- (4 mins.) Speaking partner describes stance.
- (2 mins.) Listening partner reflects back what they heard, and speaking partner corrects them if needed. (6 mins. total)
- (6 mins.) Speaker and listener switch roles.

Phase Four: Identifying, Correcting, Admitting Stereotypes (12 Minutes)

Identifying perceived stereotyping of one's position, correction of that view, and identifying nuggets of truth to the stereotype. (6 mins. for each partner)

- (2 mins.) Speaking partner identifies perceived stereotyping of their position by those critical of them, for example, "naïve" if liberal or "dogmatic" if conservative.
- (2 mins.) Speaking partner presents a correction of that view.
- (2 mins.) Speaking partner identifies nuggets of truth to the stereotype.
- (6 mins.) Speaker and listener switch roles.

Phase Five: Asking a Policy Question (10 Minutes)

In this phase, partners ask one question of each other about their respective stances. It is vital that the question be as neutral and nonpartisan as possible—just a straightforward policy question; no "gotcha," accusatory, or sarcastic questions. Ask with genuine curiosity (e.g., "Given the level of violence in our society, can you help me to understand your position on your right to openly carry a gun?" or "Can you tell me more about your belief that a white person who never owned slaves should pay reparations to people of color?")

- (5 mins.) Each partner asks one question of the other, who then responds about their respective stance.
- (5 mins.) Questioner and responder switch roles.

Phase Six: Discovery/Results (10 Minutes)

In this final phase, dialogue partners take time to reflect on and convey what they learned about themselves, their partner, and the relationship they have built. The respective partners also discuss what, if any, common ground has been achieved and what, if any, steps they will take in the future based on their dialogue.

- (5 mins.) Each partner conveys what was discovered during the dialogue. (Remember to stay in character if one is role playing a position.)
- (5 mins.) Partners switch roles.

Some questions to guide your discussion: Did you feel heard? Did your partner relate to your narrative? What was learned both about your partner and yourself? Was there any common ground achieved? Action plans? Possibilities for carrying the dialogues further?

Concluding Thoughts

The Experiential Democracy Dialogue is one way to convert presence and awe-based consciousness into a source for social good. By awe, again, I mean the humility and wonder or sense of adventure toward living; and, by presence, I mean the holding and illuminating of that which is significant within one's partner and oneself.

This format can be applied within households, classrooms, community centers (e.g., between police and community activists), the work setting, and the legislative–diplomatic setting—wherever social conflict stifles the democratic capacities to co-exist with and learn from "others" in society and wherever citizens are willing to engage in such encounters. The key here is to address not only the ideological tension between conflicting parties but the underlying ways we hold those tensions. Put another way, the question of *how* we approach each other, our facial expressions, our affects, and our physical demeanors is as important, if not more important, than the words we exchange.

It is this "whole bodied" experience that I believe is our next step for the democratic process, a step that will help us all move toward a more mature approach to the discomforts within ourselves and among others. In short, the EDD is a one-on-one dialogue format that aims not just at exchanging information about people of diverse backgrounds but cultivating the capacity to be more fully present in such interchanges—and, by implication, with oneself—so that the conditions for bridge building, discovery, and healing can be enhanced.

The world needs an intervention, just as the traumatized patient or family does. The demand for this could not be more urgent.

Chapter 13

The Price We are Now Paying
for Life-Denying Anxiety

That which I call "life-*denying* anxiety" is crushing us, and many don't see it. Take just about any of the crises facing us today, and you'll see heavy denials of anxiety. American exceptionalism and white supremacy are two examples. American exceptionalism emerges from Puritan beliefs that the break from state-controlled powers like England were destined by God, that the liberty to freely practice one's religion and to have comparative sovereignty over one's family and community was also "ordained." Some believed further that the "New World" represented a "second coming" of Christ and Christian hegemony.

However, regardless of what one believes about the religious inevitability of American exceptionalism, the actual practices too often contradicted the liberating values. Liberty and sovereignty, for example, pertained chiefly to white males; women, indigenous people, and people of color were almost completely omitted from the equation. Yet that did not deter the momentum of exceptionalist tendencies. Jefferson, for example, advocated for an "empire of liberty" that would serve as a model for the world. But part of the mission of this empire was to own slaves and double U.S. territory, regardless of its horrific costs to the original inhabitants of the land. If this form of "bulldozing" is not a denial of anxiety—the anxiety of human diversity and cultural complexity—I don't know what is.

Later American exceptionalism could be seen in the powerful belief in "manifest destiny," the belief in the "inevitability" of U.S. expansion westward, also ordained by "providence" (or God):

> The term *manifest destiny* was first used in 1845 by editor John
> L. O'Sullivan. He did not think it an especially profound phrase.
> Rather, it was buried in a long essay of his that appeared in the
> July–August issue of *The United States Magazine, and*

Democratic Review. In that essay he spoke of America's "manifest destiny" to overspread the continent allotted by Providence for the free development of our yearly multiplying millions. (from https://www.britannica.com/summary/ Manifest-Destiny-Key-Facts)

Over the past century, American exceptionalism has undergone a jarring resurgence. The tendencies of U.S. governments (Left and Right) to become involved in foreign wars and to overthrow powers that pose little threat to us (Zinn, 2003) are perhaps the most glaring examples. But American exceptionalism has taken root in many domestic forms as well, such as the White Supremacy movement. This movement, highlighted recently by the racist mass murder of black patrons in a Buffalo supermarket, holds that the so-called white race is under existential threat and that people of color, Jews, and non-European immigrants are the basis for that threat. This "Great Replacement Theory" is filtering into mainstream discourse and becoming one of the most pernicious nativist movements in decades.

It may be unfathomable that a group of white people, who have dominated the world for millennia and who continue to enjoy many powers of privilege, perceive that they are in imminent danger of being wiped out. But this is what some believe, perhaps because their world is indeed changing, and people of color and immigrants are making cultural and political strides that were unheard of in the past. But does that mean that whites will be "replaced"? Does that mean that there is no basis for dialogue and co-existence among divergent groups? Hardly, yet this is the result of the old conflation problem again. It is the fear-driven pairing of two events with no basis to do so, such as the idea that life is becoming more multicultural and, therefore, traditional life will be completely destroyed. Or, to put it alternatively, what many in the White Supremacist and Christian Nationalist movements see is the dwindling of their own powers, the major loss of jobs, the takeover of many of those jobs by nonwhite Americans (and immigrants), and the shift of culture and population toward nonwhite Americans. But what those supremacists and nationalists don't see is that, just as white Americans, nonwhite Americans live complex, multifaceted lives. They, too, have embraced America—or at least the aspiration of America—as a place of safety for their families, live-and-let-live values, and freedom from tyrannical rule.

Furthermore, many who advocate for American exceptionalism also cannot countenance foreign influence. While many American exceptionalists may not be as extreme as white supremacists on this point, the thread that connects them is a belief in U.S. superiority, and a corresponding belief that no one, especially of "foreign" descent, has a right to question that superiority—its goodness and its purity. Indeed, people who are critical about anything "American" are quickly dismissed, if not outright shunned, by such exceptionalists.

Hence, what we have here again is the vanquishing of anxiety, the absolute refusal of anxiety. Questioning and ambiguity are vanquished and so are the voices of dissent. The "solution" on the other hand, from the exceptionalist standpoint, is an almost religious reverence for tradition, or what they view as tradition. Conversely, uncomfortable thoughts, feelings, and relationships are quashed. Uncertainty and doubt are quashed; and so are wonder and discovery. There is only certitude that is left: fixations on single points of view to the utter exclusion of competing points of view.

The adoption of life-*enhancing* anxiety, by contrast—anxiety that enables living with and making the best of the mystery and depth of existence—becomes a lost project, as does civility, tolerance, creativity, and discovery. But there are so many of these lost projects today; American exceptionalism and white supremacy are but two instances of how and where they become lost.

Just consider the life-denying anxiety propelled by gun ownership; the rejection of mask-wearing due to their discomfort or political associations, as opposed to their potential to save thousands of lives; the rejection of unsettling literature or works of art; the shunning of uncomfortable ideas, be they Right or Left; the dogmatic stands on abortion; the indifference toward climate change, and the indifference toward those whose livelihoods are dependent on outdated forms of industrialization.

What all this amounts to is overidentification. It is overidentification with individual rights as opposed to the collective, or collective rights as distinct from those for individuals. It is overidentification with governmental power or private and corporate power, the stifling of free speech or the recklessness of free speech, the banishment of spirituality and religion or the invulnerability of spirituality and religion, the eradication of guns or the worship of guns, the limitlessness of free-market capitalism or the leveling of free-market capitalism, the glorifying of law enforcement or the decimating of law enforcement. You get the idea: Life-denying anxiety leads to "black and white," "either/or" living and ends in "dead-end" living.

I make no pretense of resolving this monumental human challenge in a book, but what I can say with vehemence is that this is to a large extent a result of our quick fix/instant result culture. It is also due to that primal human yearning for the unbending, the absolute, and the Answer. Moreover, that entire enterprise is easier than ever to reproduce today because of our techno-savvy world. And yet it very well may be our downfall if again we fail to pay attention to our capacity, and need, to live with and make the best of the depth and mystery of existence.

What are some practical steps we can now take to address the problem? Sensitization. We need to sensitize our youth from the start to the fullness and awesomeness of our lives—the marvels and wonders of our lives. Instead of bombarding them with either fears or fairy tales about the world's offerings, greet them with the joys of inquiry and curiosity. Greet them with manageable adventures both in story-telling and nature. Help them develop some thick skin along with the delicate, and keep the bigger picture of life's gifts astern.

In schools, we need to do the following: Stop gutting the arts and humanities for so-called information technology or "teaching to the test." Bring the arts and humanities alive both through enactments and discussion, and with subjects and objects that relate to students' contemporary lives. Invite supportive, structured discussions of difficult topics such as climate change, the pandemic, racism, and political polarization as appropriate to students' age groups. Here is a place where formats such as the Experiential Democracy Dialogues (see Chapter 12) may be especially useful. Reintroduce philosophy and critical thinking so that students can learn about the premises of given points of view and the contexts out of which they arise. In this way, they can learn to think more independently and with much greater knowledge of the moral and ethical positions that have been taken in the world and what those imply for the contemporary era. Teach, and above all, model emotional intelligence so that students can see and feel what a centered yet spirited life can open up to them. This would be a life that acknowledges our smallness and fragility but also our enormous capacity to transcend as time and circumstances allow. It is a life led by vigorous questioning of facts but also realistic acceptance of such facts as time and circumstances demand. It is a life marked by freedom to do but also freedom to be or adopt attitudes toward situations—as Viktor Frankl and Maya Angelou have shown—when time and circumstances delimit the ability to make changes in the outside world.

But perhaps most important of all, teach dynamic balance, the managing of paradoxes, and thus anxiety, so that it serves our ability to grow and discover as much as it restrains our arrogance and presumption.

Chapter 14

Urgent: The Promotion of Emotionally Restorative Relationships

Social crises are exploding today, and the mental health community needs to mobilize for action. It needs to foster the skills and resources that nurture life-enhancing, as distinct from life-destroying, anxiety. In that light, I propose that a coalition of mental health organizations develop a National Corps of Mental Health Professionals to facilitate what I call "emotionally restorative relationships." These are relationships that help people feel seen and heard and get at the root of their problems.

Specifically, I call for this Corps to provide highly structured, healing dialogues, such as those of the Experiential Democracy Dialogue and Braver Angels (described above), to address the alarming cultural and political divides in our country.

I also call for the proposed Corps to provide equitable access to longer term, emotionally restorative psychotherapy. Such a service would be especially valuable in underserved and marginalized communities where substantive services are often lacking and the urgency for such services is mounting (McPhillips, 2022, October 5). Emotionally restorative psychotherapy would also be integrative—comprising, as appropriate, medical, cognitive–behavioral, psychodynamic, and existential dimensions of practice, but with a concerted emphasis on meaningful life-changing inquiry. Such a framework would also expand the availability of therapy in public mental health clinics, homeless shelters, single room occupancy hotels (or SROs), primary and secondary schools, elder-care homes, and prisons, to name but a few of the venues in desperate need.

The Corps would also foster a wide range of relationship-building services for other sectors of our society. For example, it could expand the availability of first responders to aid police dealing with mental health emergencies. It could provide consulting services to organizations in impoverished communities and bolster the time and quality of mental health coaching for classrooms, hospitals, rehab centers, governmental and diplomatic settings—wherever such services are in greatest need today.

With regard to funding this vital project, I would make an appeal for the support of government, private industry, and others who care about the state of our society and world. Such funding in turn would generate the pilot studies, grants, and other forms of support that would help to discern the viability and long-term sustainability of Corps services. The superb resources of our mental health research, as well as applied and practice communities, will be very much needed in this timely, broad-based effort.

In concert with the above application of emotionally restorative relationships I call for a federal office of psychological advisors. This would be an office on a par with the Surgeon General but comprised of distinguished experts in psychosocial research and application. This office would complement the advocacy work that organizations such as the American Psychological Association, The American Psychiatric Association, and National Association of Social Workers are providing to inform the public about holistic and concrete ways to address the crises flaring all about us. These crises include the pandemic, political divisiveness, racism, religious and cultural tensions, alarming rates of depression, anxiety, addiction, hate crimes and violence, and consequences of war, to name but several. The office of psychological advisors would also be available 24/7 to advise the U.S. president, the various departments of government, and Congress on legislation relevant to addressing psychosocial crises.

If it seems like I'm "ringing the alarm bells" here, I emphatically am. I believe strongly that we are in a race against time in terms of the levels of despair, degradation, bipartisanship, overt and covert abuse, environmental destruction, and dysfunctional interpersonal relationships we are witnessing across our country and world. If the tide of these problems continues to swell, I'm concerned not only about our ability to impact the psychology of our challenges but also our ability to survive, to make it as a species.

Just consider the following scenarios, drawn from observations of everyday life: A Caucasian teenager is shut in his room for hours fingering his cell phone and playing video games. His parents are separated and his mother, his primary caretaker, is exhausted from low-wage jobs. The kid becomes increasingly bored, afraid of face-to-face contact, especially with young women, and misanthropic—due in no small part to the petty fights and degradations of the social media bubbles he dwells in.

Yet, what if this young man or his mother (who notices his deterioration but feels helpless to do anything about it) could access a mentor, counselor, or even depth-oriented psychotherapist at an affordable rate? Further, what if the caregiver could do outreach and actually meet with the boy in his home environment or engage in activities with him as part of the longer term therapeutic aim? What if this boy were Dylan Klebold or Eric Harris, the masterminds of the Columbine High School massacre? Or innumerable other teens who have lost their way, suffered social and developmental degradation, and received superficial "treatments," such as monthly psychiatric appointments, six-week anger management classes, or minimal contacts with a school counselor? Would they have turned out differently? A strong case could be made that they would (e.g., see Gilligan, 1999). Correspondingly, what if such a support worker were available to an African American or Hispanic child in an impoverished inner city neighborhood? Might this professional help to stem that youth's gravitation to a gang or hard drugs, or support them to find a meaningful project or skill that the youth's parents and school officials are too preoccupied to provide?

What if depth-oriented mental health staff were available to elderly residents in a homeless shelter, or struggling alcoholics in an SRO? What if "anxiety management" entailed a year-long relationship with a caregiver with superlative abilities to form an alliance with her clients, to genuinely empathize with them, and who could work with them in a holistic way that helped them obtain appropriate rehabilitation services and medicines. And what if this caregiver inspires their clients to engage in nurturing social activities, cultivate the capacity for greater autonomy, address maladaptive thought and behavioral patterns, and, perhaps most importantly (at least for many), provides a sense of safety, warmth, and receptivity that profoundly alters their outlook on life, reshapes their feelings about life.

Our culture professes to "take care of our own," to prioritize health and happiness, but in so many ways, we undermine this aspiration. Our socio-economic model has thus far prevented us from realizing how the most important elements of our aspiration—the health and well-being of our populace. the in-depth education of our youth, the education of the heart, and an enduring equitable society—are dispensed with, at least for a vast majority. The prioritization of a national corps of mental health professionals and federal office of psychological advisors, while not resolving this enormous conundrum, would in my view go a long way toward salving the wounds of the conundrum, and just possibly nudge the entire socio-economic edifice in a more human-centered, revitalizing direction.

Part 5

Spiritual and Religious Applications
of Life-Enhancing Anxiety

Overview

This segment elaborates an emerging spiritual perspective with strong implications for a renewed morality and ethics in our society. I call this perspective, which issues from life-enhancing anxiety, "enchanted agnosticism." Enchanted agnosticism takes the mystery of our existence seriously and steers us between the other two major spiritual and religious tendencies these days: post-modern relativism and premodern fundamentalism. Enchanted agnosticism acknowledges the radical uncertainty of our condition as human beings but also emphasizes a "whole-bodied" appreciation of the uncertainty, which, in turn, leads to a "faith in the inscrutable" and awe for all life and existence. In the follow-up chapter, "Museums Are My Temples: Everyday Life My Spirituality," I elaborate on how enchanted agnosticism can play out in everyday life for everyday people. Specifically, I look at the dazzling examples of "awe-based spirituality" and "life-enhancing anxiety" in museums and other secular testimonials to the "beyond." I describe my own experience of these reminders of our cosmic connection, and the exaltation I feel that is equivalent to and sometimes surpasses traditional places of veneration—such as the temple or church.

Chapter 15

A Spiritual Approach to Life-Enhancing Anxiety: Enchanted Agnosticism[1]

Let's face it: With regard to faith and ethics today, we're between a rock and a hard place. The rock is extremist–fundamentalist religion (or ideology), and the hard place is postmodern free-market anarchy (or relativism). While I am aware that these respective positions lie along a continuum of flexibility, that flexibility seems to be waning these days and the more polarized positions are taking its place.

That being said, there is an alternative to these "either/or," "black/white" extremes that have the world in a vise-grip: I call this alternative enchanted agnosticism; and elsewhere (Schneider, 2004) I have called it "awe" or "awe-based consciousness." Agnosticism has a long and many-layered history. In recent times it has come to be associated with scientific doubt (or the unverifiable); but enchanted agnosticism takes doubt, and particularly the mystery of being, a step further.

By enchanted agnosticism, I mean bedazzled uncertainty, exhilarated discernment, and enraptured curiosity; I mean the openness and skepticism of science wedded to the zeal and exaltation of religion; I mean the veneration of mystery wedded to the solemnity of responsibility. To put all this in philosophic terms, I mean our existential faith in the inscrutable. Enchanted agnostics believe that behind every institutionalized religion is a transcendent question: "But what is beyond that?" Our answer is that behind every bounded faith resides an evolving, indefinite faith. Beyond every bounded god resides an expanding, indecipherable god. Captivating as they may be, gods and goddesses, idols and icons, obsessions and fixations are but pale stand-ins for the inscrutable. Even concepts like the Absolute or Atman or the

[1] Author's Note: This chapter was originally published by *Tikkun Magazine*, Vol. 18, no. 4, July/August 2003. An expanded version of this chapter is contained in a chapter titled "Between Anarchy and Dogma: Toward a Faith in the Inscrutable" in *Rediscovery of Awe: Splendor, Mystery and the Fluid Center of Life,* Paragon House, 2004, pp. 143–162.

Void, to the degree they are decipherable, are but veneers of this mysterious power. As Paul Tillich (1952) put it in *The Courage to Be*, veneers (or pieces) of the holy must not be identified with the holy itself, which is a "God beyond God."

This radically new view of God, being, or creation is a view that trumps nihilism as it does dogma, purposelessness as it does certitude. It is a view that basks not in particular things but in the amazement, astonishment, and bewilderment of things. Whereas definable gods such as those in the Old and New Testaments, ancient myth, and popular culture tend to polarize us, either by containing and belittling us, on the one hand or inflating and exaggerating us, on the other, the inscrutable fosters wholeness—not puritan or absolute wholeness but dynamic, paradoxical wholeness. The inscrutable evokes our humility and our possibility at the same time; but instead of dictating these conditions from on high, it inspires us to negotiate them, to find our way within them. The result of this understanding is that devotees of the inscrutable are more inclined to see through their investments and be less driven by them. They are less entrapped either by false hope or false despair, and they are enlivened by a poignancy to life, an overview that heightens each attendant moment. Enchanted agnostics are the leaders-to-be of a new spiritual consciousness that some might link with a growing contemporary movement. This movement is described as the "Nones," or religiously nonaffiliated (Thompson, 2019, September). The Nones are a patchwork of atheists, agnostics, and spiritual seekers who may embrace religious sensibilities but without identifying with an organized religion or doctrine.

Three Principles
Faith in the inscrutable combines three intertwining perspectives: the magnificence of creation, the mystery of creation, and our responsibility to creation.

Magnificence
We don't need a directive or a definable god to feel the presence of divinity. The magnificence of creation demands it. That creation exists at all is magnificent, amazing, incomprehensible. So, too, all that partakes in creation must be seen as equally amazing, equally magnificent—death as well as life. This magnificence measures the span of humanity's hope and demands the tolerance that comes from being open to awe.

As Whitman (1897) reminds us:

Grand is the seen, the light, to me—grand are the stars,
Grand is the earth, and grand are lasting time and space,
And grand are their laws, so multiform, puzzling, evolutionary,
But grander far the unseen soul of me, comprehending,
    endowing all those... (p. 421)

Mystery

The flip side of magnificence is mystery. One of the greatest dangers of our age is jadedness. The more jaded we become, the less we acknowledge mystery; the less we acknowledge mystery, the more we lose touch with its current and with the inscrutable itself.

Magnificence and mystery are a pair. We cannot have magnificence without uncertainty, and we cannot have mystery without hope. This paradox is often overlooked in mystical circles, which sometimes emphasize magnificence to the detriment of mystery, but it was familiar to Tillich (2001), who points out in *The Dynamics of Faith* that mysticism neglects "the separation of man from the ultimate. There is no faith without separation" (p. 100).

With separation comes anxiety; faith must live with this sense of unease. Uncertainty reminds us of our fragility, but it also reminds us of our possibility Again, Tillich (2001):

> [F]or man is finite, and he can never unite all elements of truth in complete balance. On the other band, he cannot rest on the awareness of his finitude, because faith is concerned with the ultimate and its adequate expression. Man's faith is inadequate if his whole existence is determined by something that is less than ultimate. Therefore, he must always try to break through the limits of his finitude and reach what never can be reached, the ultimate itself. (p. 57)

Responsibility

Creation's magnificence leads us to such foundational religious concepts as respecting the stranger and venerating God. Mystery, however, leads us to responsibility, the challenge to respond. The call of magnificence can be answered by reflexive, even passive, approaches to worship. Mystery, however, calls us to what Ernest Becker (1974) describes as reflective, even dialectical worship. Once we understand the mystery of the inscrutable, we understand that each of us, as individuals, must bear the brunt of decision making.

We enchanted agnostics cannot passively defer to authority because there is no certain authority to accept our surrender. There is no marked path, no "highway to heaven," no inviolable canon. It is we who must sanctify the scripts, we who must find the path. But we are not rudderless when it comes to this process either; faith in the inscrutable does provide landmarks. The first, following magnificence, is an appreciation for all being; the second, following mystery, is an openness to what evolves; and the third, following responsibility is a challenge to respond to or discern what evolves. That which Tillich (1967) calls "listening love" (which is akin to depth therapy as well as Buber's philosophy of dialogue) is a concrete realization of the aforementioned principles. "Listening love," elaborates Tillich, is a whole-bodied immersion in a dilemma or concern. "It is a listening to and looking at the concrete situation in all its concreteness, which includes the deepest motives of the other person...." Tillich concludes, "The more seriously one has considered all the factors in a moral decision, the more one can be certain that there is a power of acceptance in the depth of life"(1967, p. 111)—and in our own lives, I might add, for the decision we risk.

The responsibility to respond compels a mutable respect, a respect that leans on humanity. Just as one can't apply a "fits all" product to a diverse and opinionated populace, one can't force a "fits all" ethic to a complex and changing existence. Instead, the principle of responsibility that is at the heart of enchanted agnosticism calls upon the deepest energies of democracy, the fullest engagements of dialogue, and the keenest perceptions of context.

Nor is the principle of responsibility a kind of "situational" ethics, as that approach is conventionally understood. Enchanted agnosticism advocates an "awe-based" situational ethics, an ethics infused by the thrill and anxiety of living and the reverence, humility, and wonder of living. While other situational ethics tend to resort to intellectual or consensus-based criteria, an awe-based ethics is ever attuned to the whole, the embodied, and the relational in its deliberations (as in listening love or person-to-person encounter).

The Way to the Inscrutable
Enchanted agnosticism, thus, is very different from the reflexive faith of disciples, or the expedient faith of marketers, or the obsessive faith of fanatics (or even G.W. Bush's faith-based education!). Faith in the inscrutable is wrought from our encounter with these and other, singular faiths. It is a faith wrought from the encounter with the myopic,

the fleeting, and the one-dimensional, a faith wrought from pain but not confined by pain. It is a faith born of deep self-inquiry, deep presence to the results of that inquiry, and deep trust in the unfolding of the results. It is a faith born of confidence that one can survive one's own intense grappling, *but* it is not just a faith in survival: It is a faith in that which permits survival to occur.

Awe-based faith entails a "giving up when there's nothing left," as Ernest Becker (1974, p. 78) intimated in his remarkable deathbed interview with Sam Keen. It is a placing of one's trust in the "tremendous creative energies of the universe" to work through and with us when we are spent. The key here is that such faith often requires that we struggle until we are spent. Struggle jolts the system, dents the armor, and jars the rails. But struggle is only the beginning. The shock and the awakening we experience are only preparatory. The next crucial question is how we pursue, engage with, and emerge from this struggle. We must learn to acknowledge, identify with, and yet somehow be more than that with which we contend.

Expediency, the catch-word of our time, is not a route to the inscrutable. It is a route to the definable, the consolable, and the delimiting. One cannot partake of the fruits of vibrancy, of the profound and the emancipating, through gimmickry. There are no tricks to cultivating awe. The danger today is that we delude ourselves into believing in such tricks, that we mistake Isaiah Berlin's (1999) jigsaw puzzle universe for the brute and throbbing one into which we are thrust. Almost every cutting-edge technology poses this danger—virtually every designer drug, genetic manipulation, and robotic innovation holds the potential for abominable self-delusion. While we can be aided and, indeed, miraculously transformed by these developments, we must not lose touch with their partiality and their envelopment by the inscrutable.

Vision
If enchanted agnosticism were to become the norm, then, how would the world look? I envision a time when enchanted agnosticism is echoed in schools and in temples, in boardrooms and in embassies, in bedrooms and in alleyways—in every human sphere. This would be a time when churches throw open their doors to mosques and mosques to synagogues, when Buddhist priests can perform sacred chanting rites before Hindu congregants, and when Jewish temples sanction Protestant services. It would be a time, perhaps, when every major denomination would regularly and on a rotating basis host every other

major denomination and yet maintain their respective identities, when families of all faiths and backgrounds would pray together, break bread together, and partake in one another's heritage.

This would also be a time when enchanted agnosticism—awe-based living—is practiced in business and diplomatic circles; when politicians and mediators and entrepreneurs model the actions they expect of others, partake in interfaith ceremonies, avail themselves of intimate interchange, and open to diverse folk traditions. Then, and only then, will the spirals of hate, of tit-for-tat, and of intercultural estrangement be stanched. Then, and only then, will conciliation have a chance.

Further, this would be a time when diplomatic and trade meetings are attended not only by policymakers but also by ethical philosophers, spiritual leaders, and organizational psychologists; when, for example, attendees participate in professionally facilitated process groups and promote frank exchanges of feeling; and when the input from scientists and philosophers matches that from legislators and generals. It would be a time when representatives can broach one another's personal fears as well as state or corporate agendas; when international relations can be spoken about in terms of interpersonal relations; and when hopes and trepidations can be coupled with predictions and averages.

Finally, this would be a time when people everywhere approach one another and our world from a stance of curiosity, wonderment, and potentially even attraction, for commensurate with the rise in enchanted agnosticism would be the corresponding rise in intra- and intercultural reassessment, trust, and cooperation; and with these developments, entire worlds will unfurl. Religious and scientific types, for example, would begin to perceive not only their respective divergences, but also their respective convergences, utility, and virtues. While adherents of doctrinal faith would reassess the value of openness and skepticism, devotees of calculation would reevaluate the legitimacy of veneration and faith; while spiritualists would rethink material realities, materialists would revisit the ethereal, poetic, and felt. Although hesitant at first, each of the respective parties would become increasingly appreciative of the others' legitimacy, lucidity, and sublimity.

Sound remote? Out-of-reach? Not necessarily. Social theorists from Carl Rogers (1986) to Michael Lerner (1996) have been promoting such interchanges for years, and many have partaken of their fruit. As more partake in The Great Conversation, fewer will pine for The Great Detonation, or The Holy Vindication; and as some invite deepening and widening, others will permit risking, opening. In short, enchanted agnosticism, the embrace of mystery, has tremendous potential to address the confusion and spiritual hunger of our lives.

In her illuminating study of religion, *The History of God*, Karen Armstrong (1993, p. 397) concludes that we in the West have reached a developmental milestone. We have witnessed the disasters of fundamentalist tyrannies and, equally, of post-Enlightenment oligarchies, and we are in need of something different. This alternative, Armstrong suggests, just might be what she calls "mystical agnosticism," which is very akin to my "enchanted agnosticism." The problem, Armstrong cautions, is that in order for such an alternative to be viable it must be "felt upon the pulse" or as Buber put it, "hallowed in the everyday." That is precisely the challenge that I pose to readers today: to feel enchanted agnosticism upon the pulse.

Chapter 16

Museums Are My Temples:
Everyday Life My Spirituality

Toward an Enchanted Agnosticism for the People

Museums are my temples. I am talking about all kinds of museums, including those of art, science, religion, history, and ethnicities. I am also talking about great cultural centers, such as libraries, theaters, and marvels of architecture, anyplace that symbolizes the humility and wonder—awe—toward all life. This sentiment has been echoed several times in recent research on the subject. As Price et al. (2021) put it, "Museums are in the business of awe" (p. 25) and "Awe is inherent in museum and cultural centers. It is one of the most commonly used descriptors of powerful guest experiences and it is often a goal of exhibit designers. Studying awe is to study one of the most profound and sublime aspects of the museum experience (p. 2)"

I think museums are the temples of the future, or should be; they remind us of the treasures that are all around us, both within and without. In this sense, museums are sanctuaries of nondogmatic inquiry, discovery, and diversity. That diversity may be uncomfortable at times, mind- or heart-stretching, but it is real, emanating from the core of the people who oversee them. The museums of the future would also be participatory. Anyone could contribute, even if the particular contribution does not end up in the permanent collection. There would be large rooms for visitors to ask questions of the curators of the museum or to participate in classes pertaining to the museum's collection. There would also be facilities for attendees to contribute to the activity of the museum. These contributions could take the form of creative works, research, discussion groups, contemplative groups, or charitable donations. All engagements would be voluntary, but decorum and respect would be emphasized, just as it is in temples and churches currently. The museums of the future would also be free, a meeting ground for the people.

As spiritual cornerstones of society, the museums would be venerated. They would be viewed as lighthouses for the sacredness of our lives, the awesomeness of our diversified journeys. They would not be rarified palaces but houses of life affirmation. They would be for everyone, for the people, for all who come to realize that they participate in something greater than themselves, greater than their kinfolk and their tribe. This transcendent dimension would point to a cosmic sensibility, like the lilting tones of a melodic voice, or the splashes of color in a van Gogh, or the depiction of human evolution from ape to homo sapiens. Correspondingly, these museum/temples would at the same time celebrate the local, the tribal, and the kindred. They would probe deep in all directions, reminding all of us of our rich and mysterious roots, our cherished rituals, and our forays into new and potentially fresh terrain. The museum/temples would remind us of our deeply personal experiences but also those we all share, the potentialities for bridge-building and commonality across the great chasms of difference and inaccessibility.

Another way to put all this is that temples (mosques, monestaries, churches, sacred spaces of all kinds) could also become museums of a sort, hallowed centers of discovery. Before taking offense at this idea, which may seem like a demotion to some, consider that this is not at all what I'm implying. Rather, I'm suggesting that via the museum, traditional places of worship could actually accentuate what they're already most concerned about (or should be)—which is alerting us to the awesomeness and preciousness of life. That is, they could become exalted places of wonder, study, and learning, just as we already have, for example, in Judaism with "Torah Study," or Islam with study of the Koran, or Buddhism and Taoism with study of scripture—but with greater emphasis. Study, inquiry, and discussion of the great teachings has been in my experience and that of many others one of the most gratifying elements of religious participation. It is precisely so because, again, it promotes community, adventure, and enlargement of view. It also promotes an aesthetic appreciation that we rarely derive from more utilitarian institutions of modern life.

Such temples of learning and inquiry could also house treasures that symbolize their teachings, just as we see in some of the most exalted traditional sanctuaries today. But they could feature even more symbolic relics, not just for idle gazing, but for meditation, and again, fresh ways of "seeing" the world—both as it has passed into history and as it is unfolding in the present. There could be wisdom-teachers from each of the traditions who are schooled not only in the principles of the given temple, but in the principles of life-philosophy that link all the great temples together—the humility and wonder or awe of living. Proceeding from this basis, each of the temples could emphasize their own form of belief system, but without imposing that form on others.

By contrast, many or all who gather around each of the temples will come to share in the fundamental tenet that life is fleeting, that we are all vulnerable, and that no one person or entity "owns" the truth. The people will observe, moreover, that we all possess pieces of the truth, and that these pieces both individually and collectively form an extraordinary tapestry. Even more fundamentally, many or most will come to realize that if we begin with the humility and wonder of living, if we begin with awe, then the most important ethical teachings suggested by the major religions will follow. Consider several from the Judeo-Christian, Islamic, Buddhist, Taoist, Native American, Hindu (and many other) traditions: "love thy neighbor as thyself," "embrace the stranger," "respect life," "respect nature," "replenish and nourish nature," "walk humbly with your creator," "be merciful," and so on. How could one not experience at least the basics of these commands if one recognizes the awesomeness and preciousness, the gift of life, right from the start? Why would one want to demean oneself or others if one feels that one is on a great adventure, a discovery-filled adventure, that will expire like a flash of light? Wouldn't one want to do everything possible to tap into this adventure, to absorb as much as possible that pays homage to this adventure and recognizes that others also desire to savor every moment of this adventure? This is the beginning of ethics, a humanistic ethics that embraces the sanctity of people, all living things, and in fact all things to the degree that such can be embraced by living, mortal creatures. This is an ethics that spurns an "us/them," "holier than thou" attitude. It spurns absolutist hierarchies and recognizes the wisdom in evolving hierarchies that are acutely aware of both their transience and incompleteness.

It takes courage to live this way, to be sure. But fundamentally it takes love because love is what supports courage to flourish. Love is the ballast for "awe wakening," for "seeing" the depth and sweep of life; otherwise we become crushed by that depth and sweep, as in a plunge without guide or equipment. Therefore, awe-based religiosity, the "museums" of sacredness begin through the processes and trials of birth, which is our plunge into a vast and unknown "sea." The question is, how is that plunge handled by caretakers, by culture, and by the native equipment of the child? How can we optimize that plunge with an awe-based canopy of humility and wonder, sense of adventure toward living, our life-philosophies and life-inquiries as well as our spiritual and religious heritages, if they truly become life-inquiries?

In the end, it will be our everyday, the art of everyday life, that evokes museum consciousness. It will be the smells and textures of human relationships, of walks through parks and woods, and even of breaths of fresh air at every moment of inhalation.

Part 6

Research on Life-Enhancing Anxiety:
What Does the Science Say?

Overview

This section considers five areas of research relevant to life-enhancing anxiety: the literature on anxiety and performance; the studies on psychological hardiness; the studies on resilience and post-traumatic growth; the data on creative and self-actualizing personalities; and the literature on the psychology of awe. Taken as a whole, this research supports invigorating, manageable anxiety—life-enhancing anxiety— as key to our health, our sanity, and our planetary survival.

Chapter 17

The Empirical Support
for Life-Enhancing Anxiety

As we have discussed in this volume, and as *lived*, anxiety can be both crippling and energizing. It can stifle us and make us despondent, or it can activate us and make us more aware, creative, and socially engaged. Depending on our personal and interpersonal backgrounds, anxiety can be experienced as awe-ful or awe-some, or some animating combination of the two. In this chapter, we look at the research that has been applied to the life-enhancing anxiety we've explored in this book. What does this research tell us about the widespread benefits of life-enhancing anxiety, and how people acquire it?

Perhaps the most cited study of the paradoxical aspects of anxiety is the so-called *anxiety/performance curve*, also known as the Yerkes-Dodson Law (Yerkes & Dodson, 1908). This "law" proposes that as arousal or anxiety go up, so, too, does general performance—say, public speaking, riding a horse, or crafting a business plan. But as anxiety continues to go up, it appears to reach a peak of diminishing returns. This is the point at which the rise in anxiety overwhelms one's capacity to focus, deliberate upon, or shape one's actions, and those abilities start to degrade. Anyone who has been in high-pressured athletic events, theatrical productions, or academic forums is likely to know this syndrome well. But the scenario goes beyond specific performances and relates to the problem of anxiety as a societal and, indeed, world problem. Too few see the need for a *modicum* of anxiety to make societies function and to enliven daily life, as we have shown. See also May (1950, 1975) and Richards (2007) for an elaboration on this point.

The benefits of life-enhancing anxiety are also borne out by the research on *psychological hardiness*. Psychological hardiness is defined as the ability to optimize commitment, control, and challenge to face life's obstacles. In this light, psychological hardiness has been shown to enhance resilience along with the depth and meaning of life (Maddi, 2006). Specifically, psychological hardiness translates into an ability to focus, for example, or to commit to a particular person or project; to achieve a manageable degree of control in the execution of that commitment; and finally to rise to the challenges of that commitment. Howard et al. (1986) also noted that psychological hardiness served as a moderator for Type A personalities. Type A personalities, according to the researchers, are ambitious, highly driven, and often irritable people. They also tend to be high-risk candidates for coronary artery disease. However, when the variable of psychological hardiness was introduced into the assessment of Type A individuals, the researchers found that those high in hardiness had fewer symptoms of physiological and emotional breakdown. Hardiness, in other words, appeared to convert destructive stress (and hence anxiety) into constructive and even resilient activation. (See also Benson & Stuart [1992] on the perception of threats as challenges for hardy individuals).

Along similar lines, the work of George Bonanno (2021) shows that resilience or what he calls the "flexibility mindset" involves facing anxiety but with an attitude of optimism, challenge, and confidence. Bonanno argues further that the flexibility mindset requires first that people face their anxiety. This is because anxiety remains menacing if one doesn't face it, and this menacing quality fuels rigidity, narrow thinking, and hopelessness. The encounter with one's anxiety, on the other hand, at the least enables one to see it for what it is, which is often less threatening than what one fantasizes it to be. It also enables one to see dimensions of the anxiety, such as a need to rediscover one's abilities or to fight for what one believes in, that one may not have seen prior to the encounter. This flexibility mindset is associated with three other qualities that distinguish resilient people: *optimism,* the sense of hope that life can be better; a *challenge orientation*, the recognition that crises can also be opportunities to regain skills that restore vitality and meaning to one's life; and *confidence*, the sense that one "can do it," coupled with the pride that reinforces the latter sense.

While studies of resilience and hardiness emphasize the ability to "snap back" or return to a pre-traumatized state of health, studies of *post-traumatic growth* stress the ability not just to weather difficult circumstances but to actually benefit and grow from adversity (Tedeschi & Calhoun, 1995). Thus, post-traumatic growth studies have looked at people who converted their anxiety into creative projects, innovative forms of work, expanded and deepened friendships, love relationships, and societal commitments.

For example, in the case of Rank's studies of artists, or the "artist-type," the courage to grapple with and convert life's trials into something meaningful to one's self and those affected by one is central (see also May, 1975). Rank (1989) distinguishes the "neurotic" from the artist on the basis of tolerance for and capacity to shape one's anxiety into something that contributes to the welfare of oneself and others. Another way to put this is that the artist develops the fortitude to *respond to* rather than merely react against the sorrows and difficulties of his or her world; this response takes the form of a project, a craft, a business, or calling that enriches those it touches. But, again, courage is the keynote here, the courage to live with and make the best of the depth and mystery of living, as I indicated earlier in this volume. This means that one can suffer in the most depraved circumstances—such as being raped in the case of Maya Angelou, dying of ALS as in the case of Stephen Hawking, or even languishing in a Nazi death camp as in the case of Viktor Frankl—and find one's way to creative and alternative paths.

Of course, the ability to transform woundedness into constructive outlooks does not generally arise from thin air. As Alice Miller (1990) and D.W. Winnicott (1965) have elaborated, people often need a "helpful witness" or "good enough mother" to develop the fortitude— or "transmuting internalization," as Kohut (1977) put it—to withstand the scary places in their lives. That which Laing has called "ontological security," or security with being itself, is often transmitted through a close other who has cultivated that ability in themselves. The close other then becomes a model for the developing child to emulate and draw upon during their own times of stress. Accordingly, resilient people have often been gifted with contact with other resilient people who have demonstrated that one can not only co-exist with the unsettling but can intensively transform it. And this transformation can lead to new sensitivities and capacities, a fuller and more dynamic life. The old wound as both prison and opening is relevant here, and so is the capacity to be present above and beyond one's crippling identification.

The courage to grapple with the paradoxes of living is also well illustrated by Maslow's self-actualizing subjects. These subjects as Maslow (1968) eloquently explained were "all integrators, able to bring separates and even opposites together into unity" (p. 140). In trying to parse out the basis of this ability, Maslow proposed that self-actualizers had relatively less fear than other people. "They were certainly less enculturated," he said; "less afraid of what other people would say or demand or laugh at." "Perhaps more important," he went on, self-actualizing people showed "a lack of fear of their own insides, of their own impulses, emotions, thoughts....This approval and acceptance of their own deeper selves then made it possible to perceive bravely the real nature of the world and also made their behavior more spontaneous....They could let themselves be flooded by emotion" and yet maintain a sense of "wholeness" (pp. 140-141).

But perhaps the most important research on life-enhancing anxiety, as I have intimated in this book, derives from the voluminous investigations of the sense of awe toward living. By awe toward living, I mean a renewed spiritual outlook. This outlook comprises humility (or recognition of one's vulnerability) coupled with a sense wonder (or recognition of one's boldness to inquire, discover, and participate in something much greater than oneself). The development of a sense of awe toward life is also a critical basis for a renewed sense of ethics, for who would want to destroy oneself or others if one becomes acutely aware of how precious and fleeting our lives are? Who would want to degrade others and the planet if one feels like one participates in the evolution of others and the planet, not only for one's own lifetime but for lifetimes beyond oneself?

These studies of the awe toward life stretch from penetrating qualitative inquiries—such as those by Rank (1941), Maslow (1971), and May (1991); see also Becker (1973), Buber (1970), Tillich (1952), Heschel (1951), and Schneider (2009)—to the quantitative experimental investigations of researchers such as Keltner and Haidt (2003), Yaden et al., (2018), and many others (see Kaufman, 2021). The gist of these studies shows that by facing and grappling with their anxieties, people not only can become energized by particular parts of life, but they can become energized by the very process of living itself. Another way to put this is that the more people can face and grapple with the contrasts and contradictions of their lives, the greater the likelihood that they will experience the humility and wonder, sense of adventure—in short, awe—of everyday life. Another implication of these studies is that the more people avoid encountering contrasts and contradictions in their lives, the greater the likelihood that they will become rigidified, absolutist, and polarized. Indeed, that which I call "the polarized mind," which is the fixation on single points of view to the utter exclusion of competing points of view, is precisely a maneuver of avoidance. Yet that avoidance is also precisely what fosters grandiosity and destructiveness, the hallmarks of so much damage and destruction today

The wealth of recent research on the psychology of awe also reinforces the pairings of anxiety and freedom, apprehension and wonderment that are at the crux of life-enhancing anxiety. For example, Keltner and Haidt (2003) defined awe as a sense of vastness that cannot be assimilated (that is, integrated into existing schemas) but that could potentially be accommodated (that is, integrated into new schemas) given time and circumstance. They followed their classic study with many subsequent studies, augmented by many subsequent researchers, and found that when people were primed for a sense of awe (e.g., by taking walks in nature, observing cosmic events, sitting before sunsets or sprawling landscapes), they tended to feel more fulfilled than when they were primed for "happiness." They also tended to score higher on scales of life satisfaction, volunteerism, gratitude, altruism, creativity, and concern about the environment than those who were not exposed to awe-inducing stimuli (Kaufman, 2021; Yaden et al, 2018).

There is also a growing body of in-depth qualitative studies of awe that affirm, and in some cases, go beyond the quantitative research sparked by Keltner and Haight. This literature also stresses the impact of awe across people's lifetimes and diverse family, cultural, and religious contexts. My own research on awe, for example, accented the anxiety polarity as much as the polarity of boldness and exuberance (Schneider, 2009). The majority of participants in my study had derived from very trying circumstances in their lives—from growing up with a psychotic parent to participating in gangs, to abusing mind-altering drugs, to laboring with stage four cancer and more. Yet these people were able to turn their lives around by experiencing the sense of humility and wonder and adventure that characterizes awe. To put it more directly, many of my participants either met or emulated people who inspired them to see the "more" in their circumstances beyond the narrow or petty identifications with which they were conditioned and to hold that "more" in a fresh outlook toward life. This outlook acknowledged the suffering they'd experienced but also the capacity to draw on that difficulty to discover fresh ways to think, feel, and be. Here, for example, is what one interviewee, Mark, had to say about the psychotherapeutic transformation of awe, his transformation:

> Awe is in one special sense the excitement of participation.... Awe befriends depth psychotherapy—not by promising to remove all pain, rather by addressing with reverence the pained person, not by eradicating his conflict. Instead by paying attention to the role of friction and combat as the exile's resolve to cross the desert; not by encouraging the positive, more by

paying attention to who one is, finally, not by dismissing sin, but more important, by seeking fellowship within the tragedy of alienation and estrangement. (p.117)

What this and other accounts amount to is the capacity for life-enhancing anxiety to renew many rigidified states, many tired assumptions, and many embittered souls. It opens the way for new internalizations that allow for much more consciousness about the rich offerings of life, including those that appear damaging at first but that later, through concerted effort, become part and parcel of something much larger and more rewarding.

Epilogue

The ironic message of this book is that we are bathed in anxiety precisely because we refuse, and have refused for millennia, to face anxiety. We're more isolated, angry, withdrawn, addicted, obsessive, compulsive, phobic, racist, robotic, chaotic, and tyrannical precisely because we have spurned earlier capacities for life-enhancing anxieties that could have preempted the later ones. Why do you think nations so often go to war, parents smother their children, or, on the other hand, mortify them? Why do people of certain skin colors berate people of other skin colors? Or creeds, cultures, nations, classes degrade other creeds, cultures, nations, and classes? How can we have such hatred and disrespect for people we hardly know? Why do we follow the Stalins, Hitlers, Maos, and Pol Pots of this world much more readily than we do leaders like Socrates, Rumi, Jesus, Moses, King, Gandhi, Mandela, and Lao Tzu? We admire the latter and follow some of their teachings, to be sure, but we don't typically live their teachings as we live and emulate the teachings of tyrants, moguls, and celebrities.

We are constantly driven by anxiety rather than learning to live with it, make the best of it, enable it to show us fresh possibilities for development. We continually spurn discovery as we do humility, because to animate either is to acknowledge the discomfort that goes along with full humanness, paradoxical humanness. Yet, as a result, we too often miss the rewards of that full and paradoxical path.

Correspondingly, much of humanity has committed a monumental mistake throughout history, and that is our failure to attend to the awesomeness of our predicament. What I mean is that repeatedly we have encountered crises, whether human or cosmic, that open us to the abysses of our condition (our groundlessness); but instead of facing these crises and working them through, we too often deny them and design our lives around the pretense that they don't exist. We design our lives to avoid any hint of the insignificance, smallness, fragility evoked by the crises and develop a pseudo-significance or absolute in its place. This, again, is what I call "the polarized mind." The antidote to this polarization is a new appreciation of life's awesomeness. It is an appreciation shown by all the great wisdom traditions throughout history, deriving from some of those same cultures that were formerly polarized. I'm thinking here of nondogmatic, philosophically and spiritually informed groups such as the Socratic philosophers of ancient Greece, the meditative cultures in the Near and far East, and the depth psychotherapy communities and practices in contemporary America.

When will we learn that there ain't no answer, with a capital "A," that there are only great questions and marvelous but temporary places to land. If we can absorb life with our whole bodily being, find ground within groundlessness, and make the best of the depth and mystery of existence, we will have accomplished a great feat. From that vantage point, we can reach far ahead of the norm that anchors too many of us to the terra firma of rules and regulations, on the one hand, or the airy ideals of boundlessness and perfection, on the other. If we attend closely, life-enhancing anxiety will help us navigate the perilous waters of both.

Appendix A

Prefatory Note
By Kirk Schneider

What follows are the complete, though lightly edited, progress notes that my psychoanalyst, the late Dr. Edward Schiff, provided to me on August 13th, 1991. I visited Dr. Schiff several days before his delivery of these notes in the context of a book I was working on at the time—*Horror and the Holy: Wisdom-Teachings of the Monster Tale* (Schneider, 1993). I also, frankly, was simply curious about whether Dr. Schiff still had a record of his work with me and what that record contained. Given that I was 35-five-years old at the time of my request, as well as a practicing psychologist and writer, Dr. Schiff very generously agreed to look into his files and see what he could find. To our mutual surprise, Dr. Schiff found a little ragged notebook containing his observations at the start of my analysis.

While much of this record comprised his observations of my parents' interactions with me approximately three-and-a-half years after my brother's death (I had just turned six at the time they referred me to Dr. Schiff), a notable part also revealed Dr. Schiff's observations of me. My recollection (which my mother later confirmed) was that I saw Dr. Schiff for about a year following these initial observations, and that his work with me was life transforming. That being said, and as Dr. Schiff acknowledges in his evaluation summary provided below, there may be a few inaccuracies in his recollection of me. But the gist of what he says seems to me to be highly accurate; and this, too, was confirmed by subsequent discussions with my mother. (My father, it should be noted, had passed away at age 53, eleven years before my receipt of this record; and my mother died at the age of 90 just two years ago.)

Most important, my hope is that this record will be of solace to others who struggle with trauma. Again, I was extremely fortunate to have received the insight and understanding of all involved in this ordeal. Although, as will be seen, my parents battled mightily with their own inner demons and sometimes projected these onto me, in the long run they were highly supportive of me and my quest to find a life of meaning and depth. Indeed, it is clear to me that my parents were intent on this goal from the start; but, looking back, I can only begin to grasp how trying the whole ordeal must have been for them. No one can wrap their mind around the loss of a child, and on top of that, as Dr. Schiff's summary makes evident, they had very different life philosophies and were headed for an eventual divorce.

Finally, I realize that by revealing these intimate observations, I am to some degree putting my professional reputation on the line. Yet my overriding feeling is that it is worth the risk, particularly when doing so may assist others to relate to and learn from the disclosure. To be sure, there have been instances where psychologists and other mental health professionals have revealed intimate details of their lives, but they are all too rare in my view. On the contrary, we too often hold ourselves out as "holier than thou," and that is no way to reach people on a human level. Nor is it real, as the notes below make plain. But I hope they also make plain that with the support of a patient, thoughtful witness even the deepest cuts can heal—and that we need many more such witnesses in our world.

In sum, the record below is raw. It has many painful moments both for me and I imagine some readers who know me or relate strongly to the material. Yet again, it is how real lives are sometimes lived—and need to be faced. I hope then that this record will demonstrate, in concert with this book, that some of the profoundest anxiety we can experience can eventually be recast--or at least coped with--in the light of an enlarged view.

Notes from the Psychiatric Evaluation of Kirk Schneider
[At Six Years Old]

Edward Schiff, MD
July,1962

Both parents appeared for the first interview. They identified Kirk's problem as being a thumb sucker with shreds of an old blanket, which he soaks in urine (even after mother washed it). Kirk is enuretic every night.

This is an apparently withdrawn child ever since the death of his brother from myocarditis when Kirk was almost three years of age. Kelly had been sick for almost 10 months and died in Boston where he had been taken for consultation after an initial workup at Babies and Children's [Hospital]. Kirk had been left during this time. The mother left entirely during this period in a psychological sense. She had Kirk cared for during Kelly's illness by her own mother, who, according to Kirk's father, was quite hysterical. The mother, according to her and her husband, was in a depression for about four years after the death of Kelly. Kelly had been a brilliant child. He talked well and was considered to be a star. He was the light of his mother's eye. Mother was and is a TV commercial [spokesperson]. Kirk had a good relationship with his brother prior to his death and with his mother, but it was entirely secondary to Kelly. The father generally assumed the mother role with Kirk. The father would take Kirk, who was quite regressed at this time, to movies—Snow White, for example, plus other scary movies. The mother, following Kelly's illness, because of her rejection of Kirk was then rejected by Kirk. According to my notes, the boy was very angry with his mother. This began to change somewhat when she had been in psychotherapy. [This is because] she was able to work more effectively with him, could talk with him, and be more of a mother. She could communicate with him, which she could not [do] previously because of Kelly....

The father has gone over and over with Kirk how Kelly died and has been absolutely honest with him and attempted to answer all his questions. Father has encouraged Kirk to be outgoing. Father is a teacher in the Euclid [Ohio] school system who believes in an educational philosophy of allowing the child to express his feelings. For example, if the child is angry, talk with him; if the child wants to hit, let him hit. The mother, on the other hand, was all for verbalization but not the acting-out part of the aggression. The parents had many arguments about this kind of thing. Another example of the difference of opinion was when Kirk was taken to Euclid Beach [Amusement] Park and was very frightened. Mother was in agreement with the father that [they] were miles apart in their understanding of Kirk and how all this affected him. Father tends to be intellectual; mother, at long last, following her psychotherapy, is able to feel....

It is not clear why the parents have brought Kirk at this point when he has obviously been quite disturbed for years. There is obviously much disagreement between the parents. The mother took off for a week by herself after Kelly's death, which likely made things more difficult, and several times a similar trip has been taken since....

I thought, as I understood my notes, that the mother's depression without doubt has played a major part in the way she expresses her anger at her husband and at Kirk's refusal to let her cuddle or kiss him....Kirk regressed quite a bit after Kelly's death and cried for days. Gradually he came out of it with his father's help....

At the second interview with the parents, it was clear there was a major disagreement about the overstimulation proffered by the father. Father, for example, would toss Kirk in the air. Kirk would sleep with father or with both parents....Mother felt father allowed the child to go too far in the way he acts....

There needs to be discussion (from my notes) how Kirk handles his symptoms. Father doesn't feel he's abnormal, although there is indication from both parents that Kirk is obsessed with the idea of death and dying. It was difficult to do anything with the parents because they disagree so much about everything. Father disagrees most with mother, who is now taking a more feelingful approach. Father quotes Erich Fromm. The disagreement between the parents is important, and for this reason there has to be discussion of the effect of the mother's psychotherapy and her change, particularly.

The interview with Kirk took place on 30 July 1962. A very handsome, extremely verbal child, he was unable to come into the interview room alone. He was much too frightened. But after 20 minutes he could let his mother go and could talk of how scared he was despite the fact that he had been well prepared. The theme of the talk was how scared he was of witches, and he drew something about witches.... He believes witches have a magic way of harming children. He also was frightened, I think of horses.... I'm unclear what this means but he had a fantasy that whatever he was talking about could kill children; witches were dangerous and he used to think his mother had been a witch. He seems less scared of her now. He is convinced she is not a witch, but if daddy's away and he's home alone with mother, he's frightened. It has to do with either the witches are bums or stronger than mommy. He also dreams of witches. He told a long dream about witches and brooms and how frightened he was and how he ran and swam rivers and all witches died until he went to New York. (This is unclear but obviously a scary dream having to do with witches, excitement, and being away with his mother). When Kirk was in New York there are no witches. He talked something about Cinderella, which I didn't quite understand, and also about Sleeping Beauty, a movie he had seen about four years ago.... Kirk watches TV a lot.... I asked [Kirk] if anything else happened four years ago. He denied anything had happened, and I brought up the fact I knew his brother had died four years ago.

I felt Kirk was a very bright child who was terribly frightened and excited by witches and things between legs—mother, father, primal scene, probably.... He could hardly stop talking about many of these things. He related extremely well. He was talking about many things he had observed, a confusion about death and dying, witches, primal scene, etc.

As I recall, my recommendation was that Kirk needed psychotherapy or perhaps even analysis to try to work through the traumatic events in his life, in addition to the ordinary overstimulated and exciting things going on around him.... As I recall (I'm not entirely sure) I think I came down on the side of analysis rather than psychotherapy because I thought Kirk likely had rather major unconscious internalized conflicts.

These are the notes as I have reconstructed them. I'm sure there are inaccuracies but it's likely there's enough to piece together any information you [Kirk] would like to include in whatever it is you're writing.

Edward Schiff, MD
August 12, 1991

References

Alloy, L. & Abramson, L. (1988). Depressive realism: Four theoretical perspectives. In L. Alloy (Ed.), *Cognitive processes in depression* (pp. 223–265). Guilford.

Armstrong, K. (1993). *The history of God*. Ballantine.

Bahktin, M. (1984). *Rabelais and his world* (H. Iswolsky, Trans.). Indiana University Press.

Barber, B.R. (1995). *Jihad vs. McWorld: How globalism and tribalism are reshaping the world*. Ballantine.

Bar-On, D. (1993). First encounters between children of survivors and children of perpetrators of the holocaust. *Journal of Humanistic Psychology, 33*(4), 6–14.

Batchelor, S. (1998). *Buddhism without beliefs*. Riverhead Press.

Becker, E. (1967). *Beyond alienation*. George Braziller.

Becker, E. (1973). *The denial of death*. Free Press.

Becker, E. (1974, April). The heroics of everyday life: A theorist of death confronts his own end. In *Psychology Today*, interview with Sam Keen.

Becker, E. (1975). *Escape from evil*. Free Press.

Benson, H. & Stuart, E.M. (1992). *The wellness book: The comprehensive guide to maintaining health and treating stress-related illness*. Birch Lane Press.

Berlin, I. (1999). *The roots of romanticism*. Princeton University Press.

Bodenhausen, G., Kramer, G., & Susser, K. (1994). Happiness and stereotypic thinking in social judgment. *Journal of Personality and Social Psychology, 66(4)*, 621–632.

Bonanno, G. (2021). *The end of trauma: How the new science of resilience is challenging how we think about PTSD*. Basic Books.

Brown, A., Held,T., Ramchand, R., Palimaru, A., Weilant, S., Rhoads, A, & Hiatt, L. (2021). Violent extremism in America: Interviews with former extremists and their families on radicalization and deradicalization. *Rand Corporation Study* https://www.rand.org/content/dam/rand/pubs/research_reports/RRA1000/RRA1071-1/RAND_RRA1071-1.pdf

Buber, M. (1970). *I and thou*. Scribners.

Bugental, J. (1987). *The art of the psychotherapist*. Norton.

Burke, E. (1757/1998). *A philosophical enquiry into the sublime and beautiful*. Penguin.

Camus, A. (1991). *The plague*. Vintage.

Elkins, D. (1998). *Beyond religion: A personal program for building a spiritual life outside the walls of traditional religion*. Quest Books.

Fanon, F. (2004). *The wretched of the earth*. Grove Press.

Fatemi, M. (2021). *The psychology of inner peace: Discovering heartfulness*. Cambridge University Press.

FeldmanHall, O., & van Baar, J. (2022). A tale of two perspectives: Reply to Schneider (2022). *American Psychologist, 77*(5), 712–713. https://doi.org/10.1037/amp0001022

Firestone, R. (2022). *Challenging the fantasy bond: A search for personal identity and freedom.* American Psychological Association Press.

Foucault, M. (1973). *Madness and civilization: A history of insanity in the age of reason.* Vintage.

Frankl, V. (1992). *Man's search for meaning: An introduction to logotherapy.* Beacon Press.

Fredrickson, B., & Losada, M. (2005). Positive affect and the complex dynamics of human flourishing. *American Psychologist, 60,* 678–686.

Friedman, H., & Brown, N. (2018). Implications of debunking the "critical positivity ratio" for humanistic psychology: Introduction to special issue. *Journal of Humanistic Psychology, 58*(3), 239–261. https://doi.org/10.1177/0022167818762227

Fromm, E. (1964). *The heart of man.* Harper-Colophon.

Georganda, E. T. (2020). Eros, Thanatos, and the awakening of Oistros: Being in love with life and "our" world. *The Humanistic Psychologist, 48*(2), 133–141. https://doi.org/10.1037/hum0000142

Gilligan, J. (1999). *Violence: Reflections on our deadliest epidemic.* Jessica Kingsley.

Goldhagen, D. (1996). *Hitler's willing executioners: Ordinary Germans and the Holocaust,* Alfred A. Knopf.

Grof, S. & Grof, C. (1989). *Spiritual emergency: When personal transformation becomes a crisis.* Tarcher.

Greene, B. (2021). *Until the end of time: Mind, matter, and our search for meaning in an evolving universe.* Vintage.

Haidt, J. (2013). *The righteous mind: Why good people are divided by politics and religion.* Knopf-Doubleday.

Handler, R. (2006, January/February). Twenty weeks of happiness: Can a course in positive psychology change your life? *Psychotherapy Networker.*

Harari, Y. (2015). *Sapiens: A brief history of humankind.* HarperCollins.

Hawkins, E. (2022, January). Does our approach at braver angels work? https://braverangels.org/does-our-approach-at-braver-angels-work/

Heschel, A. (1951). *Man is not alone. A philosophy of religion.* Farrar, Straus & Giroux.

Howard, J., Cunningham, D., & Rechnitzer, P. (1986). Personality (hardiness) as a moderator of job stress and coronary risk in Type A individuals: A longitudinal study. *Journal of Behavioral Medicine, 9,* 229-244.

Intelligence Report. (1999, Fall). Newsletter of the Southern Poverty Law Center. Issue 66.

James, W. (1902/1936). *The varieties of religious experience.* Modern Library.

Jamison, K. (1993). *Touched by fire: Manic-depressive illness and the artistic temperament.* Free Press.

Jung, C. (1966). *Two essays on analytical psychology.* (R.F.C. Hull, Trans.). Princeton University Press.

Kaufman, B. (2021). *Transcend: The new science of self-actualization.* Random House.

Kaufmann, W. (1968). *Nietzsche: Philosopher, psychologist, antichrist.* Vintage.

Kaufmann, W. (1975). *From Dostoyevsky to Sartre.* New American Library.

Keltner, D., & Haidt, J. (2003). Approaching awe: A moral, spiritual and aesthetic emotion. *Cognition and Emotion, 17*(2), 297–314.

Kohut, H. (1977). *The restoration of the self.* International Universities Press.

Kramer, R. (2019). *The birth of relationship therapy: Carl Rogers meets Otto Rank.* Psychosozial-Verlag.

Kramer. R. (in press). Discovering the existential unconscious: Rollo May encounters Otto Rank. *The Humanistic Psychologist* https://doi.org/10.1037/hum0000272.

Kruglanski, A.W., Gelfand, M. & Gunaratna, R. (2012). Terrorism as a means to end and end: How political violence bestows significance. In P. R. Shaver, & M. Mikulincer, (Eds.), *Meaning, mortality, and choice: The social psychology of existential concerns* (pp. 203-212). American Psychological Association. https://doi.org/10.1037/13748-000

Laing, R. (1967). *The politics of experience.* Vintage.

Laing, R. (1969). *The divided self: An existential study in sanity and madness.* Penguin.

Lagercrantz, H. (2016). The stress of being born and first breaths. *Infant Brain Development.* DOI 10.1007/978-3-319-44845-9_5

Lee, B. (2019). *The Dangerous Case of Donald Trump: 37 Psychiatrists and Mental Health Experts Assess a President - Updated and Expanded with New Essays.* Thomas Dunne Books.

Lerner, M. (1996). *The politics of meaning: Restoring hope and possibility in an age of cynicism.* Addison-Wesley.

Longrich, N. (2020, November). Did Neanderthals go to war with our ancestors? *The Conversation.* BBC online. https://www.bbc.com/future/article/20201102-did-neanderthals-go-to-war-with-our-ancestors)

Lovecraft, H.P. (1973). *Supernatural horror in literature.* Dover.

Maddi, S. R. (2006). Hardiness: The courage to grow from stresses. *The Journal of Positive Psychology, 1*(3), 160–168. https://doi.org/10.1080/17439760600619609

Maslow, A. (1968). *Toward a psychology of being.* Van Nostrand.

Maslow, A. (1971). *The farther reaches of human nature.* Penguin.

May, R. (1950). *The meaning of anxiety.* Pocket Books.

May, R. (1969). *Love and will.* Norton.

May, R. (1975). *The courage to create.* Norton.

May, R. (1981). *Freedom and destiny.* Norton.

May, R. (1991). *The cry for myth.* Norton.

May, R. (1995). The wounded healer. In K. Schneider & R. May (Eds.) *The psychology of existence* (pp. 98–102). McGraw-Hill https://create.mheducation.com/createonline/index.html#preview].

McPhillips, D. (2022, October 5). 90 percent of U.S. adults say the United States is experiencing a mental health crisis, CNN/KFF poll finds. CNN/Kaiser Family Foundation Poll. https://www.cnn.com/2022/10/05/health/cnn-kff-mental-health-poll-wellness

Mikulincer, M., & Shaver, P. (2012). Helplessness: A hidden liability associated with failed defenses against awareness of death (pp.37–53). *Meaning, mortality, and choice: The social psychology of existential concerns.* American Psychological Association. https://doi.org/10.1037/13748-000

Miller, A. (1990). *The untouched key: Tracing childhood trauma in creativity and destructiveness.* Doubleday.

Montuori, M., & Purser, R. (2015). Humanistic psychology in the workplace. In K. Schneider, J. Pierson, & J. Bugental (Eds.), *The handbook of humanistic psychology: Theory, research, and practice* (2nd ed.; pp. 723-734). Sage.

More in Common (2019). The perception gap. *More in Common.* (Retrieved 2/15/20 at https://perceptiongap.us/).

Moss, D. (2015). The roots and genealogy of humanistic psychology. In K. Schneider, F. Pierson, & J. Bugental (Eds.) *The handbook of humanistic psychology: Theory, practice, and research* (pp. 3–18). Sage.

Moyers, B. (Executive Producer; 1988, March 28). Facing evil—A conference sponsored by the Institute for the Humanities. New York: *Public Affairs Television.*

Moyers, B. (2005, January 30). Harvard commencement address. (Survey based on a 2002 Time–CNN poll.)

Nagy, E., Pilling, K., Watt, R., Pal, A., & Orvos, H. (1978). Neonates' responses to repeated exposure to a still face. PLoS One. 2017; 12(8): e0181688. https://doi.org/10.1371/journal.pone.0181688

Nietzsche, F. (1960). *Thus spake Zarathustra.* (A. Tillie, Trans.). J.M. Dent & Sons.

Otto, R. (1923/1958). *The idea of the holy.* Oxford University Press.

Payne, J. (2005, March 16). Obesity spreads across the Atlantic to Europe. *San Francisco Chronicle,* p. A-12.

Piaget, J. (2006). *The origin of intelligence in the child.* Routledge.

Price, C., Greenslit, J., Applebaum, L., Harris, N., Segovia, G., Quinn, K. & Krogh-Jespersen, S. (2021, April 26). Awe & Memories of Learning in Science and Art Museums. http://www.tandfonline.com/10.1080/10645578.2021.1907152, retrieved October 4, 2022 from https://resources.informalscience.org/sites/default/files/Awe%202021%20-%20Preprint.pdf

Pollan, M. (2018). *How to change your mind: What the new science of psychedelics teaches us about consciousness, dying, addiction, depression, and transcendence.* Penguin.

Rank, O. (1924). *The trauma of birth.* Dover.

Rank, O. (1936). *Will therapy.* Knopf.

Rank, O. (1941). *Beyond psychology.* Dover.

Rank, O. (1989). *Art and Artist.* Norton. (Originally published in 1932)

Richards, R. (2007). *Everyday creativity and new views of human nature: Psychological, social and spiritual perspectives.* American Psychological Association Press.

Rifkin, J. (2005). *The European dream.* Los Angeles: Tarcher.

Robin, C. (2001, December 16). Closet-case studies. *New York Times Magazine*, pp. 23–24.

Rogers, C.R. (1986). The rust workshop: A personal overview. *Journal of Humanistic Psychology, 26*(3), 23–45.

Rorty, R. (1991). Heidegger, Kundera, and Dickens. In R. Rorty (Ed.) *Essays on Heidegger and others.* Cambridge University Press.

Schachtel, E. (1959). *Metamorphosis: On the development of affect, perception, attention, and memory.* Basic Books.

Schneider, K. J. (1990). *The paradoxical self: Toward an understanding of our contradictory nature.* Humanity Books. (2nd ed. published in 1999.)

Schneider, K. J. (1993). *Horror and the holy: Wisdom-teachings of the monster tale.* Open Court.

Schneider, K. J. (1999). The fluid center: A third millennium vision of culture. *The Humanistic Psychologist, 27*(1), 114–130.

Schneider, K. J. (2003, July/August). Enchanted agnosticism. *Tikkun Magazine.*

Schneider, K. J. (2004). *Rediscovery of awe: Splendor, mystery and the fluid center of life.* St. Paul: Paragon House.

Schneider, K. J. (2009). *Awakening to awe: Personal stories of profound transformation.* Jason Aronson.

Schneider, K. J. (2013). *The polarized mind: Why it's killing us and what we can do about it.* University Professors Press.

Schneider, K. J. (2015). *Existential-Integrative psychotherapy: Guideposts to the core of practice.* Routledge.

Schneider, K. J. (2020). *The depolarizing of America: A guidebook for social healing.* University Professors Press.

Schneider, K. J. (2022). Broadening the perspective on the polarized mind: Commentary on van Baar and FeldmanHall (2022). *American Psychologist, 77,* 710–711.

Schneider, K. J. & May, R. (1995). *The psychology of existence: An integrative, clinical perspective.* McGraw-Hill.

Schneider, K. J., Pierson, J., & Bugental, J. F. T. (2015). *The handbook of humanistic psychology: Theory, practice, and research.* Sage.

Schwarzbaum, L. (2009, May). Cannes report: Lars von Trier's Antichrist: The closest film to a scream. *Inside Movies.* *http://insidemovies.ew.com/2009/05/17/cannes-report-a/*

Shedler, J., Mayman, M., & Manis, M. (1993). The illusion of mental health. *American Psychologist, 48,* 1117–1131.

Shedler, J. (2012). The efficacy of psychodynamic psychotherapy. In R. A. Levy, J. S. Ablon, & H. Kächele (Eds.), *Psychodynamic psychotherapy research: Evidence-based practice and practice-based evidence* (pp. 9–25). Humana Press – Springer. https://doi.org/10.1007/978-1-60761-792-1_2.

Shirer, W. (1960). *The rise and fall of the third reich.* Simon & Schuster.

Shelley, M. (1818/1981). *Frankenstein.* Bantam.

Solomon, S., Greenberg, J., & Pyszczynski, T. (2015). *The worm at the core: The role of death in life.* Random House.

Sontag, S. (2009). *Styles of radical will.* Penguin. Excerpt retrieved September 25, 2022 from https://www.maramarietta.com/eroticism-in-fiction/sontag-pornographic-imagination/

Stambor, Z. (2005, June). Self-reflection may lead independently to creativity, depression. *American Psychological Association Monitor, 36,*13.

Stolorow, R. (2007). *Trauma and human existence: Autobiographical, psychoanalytic, and philosophical reflections.* Routledge.

Tedeschi, R. & Calhoun, L. (1995). *Trauma and transformation: Growing the aftermath of suffering.* Sage.

Thompson, D. (2019, September 26th). Three decades ago, America lost its religion. Why? *The Atlantic.* https://www.theatlantic.com/ideas/archive/2019/09/atheism-fastest-growing-religion-us/598843/).

Tillich, P. (1952). *The courage to be.* Yale University Press.

Tillich, P. (1963). *Kierkegaard's existential theology.* Part 2. (CD recording T577 123, Paul Tillich Compact Disk Collection). Richmond, VA: Union PSCE.

Tillich, P. (1967). *My search for absolutes.* Simon & Schuster.

Tillich, P. (2001). *The dynamics of faith.* Perennial.

Tronick, E. (1989). Emotions and emotional communication in infants. *American Psychologist. 44*(2),112–119.

van der Kolk, B, (2014). *The body keeps the score: Brain, mind, and body in the healing of trauma.* Penguin.

Wampold, B. (2008, February 4). Existential-integrative psychotherapy: Coming of age [Review of the book *Existential-integrative psychotherapy: Guideposts to the core of practice*]. *PsycCRITIQUES-Contemporary Psychology: APA Review of Books, 53* (No. 6).

Waterman, A. S. (2013). The humanistic psychology–positive psychology divide: Contrasts in philosophical foundations. *American Psychologist, 68*(3), 124–133. https://doi.org/10.1037/a0032168

Whitman, W. (1897). *Leaves of grass.* Small, Maynard, and Company. Retrieved from https://tile.loc.gov/storage-services/public/gdcmassbookdig/leavesofgrass01whit/leavesofgrass01whit.pdf

Winnicott, D. (1965). *The maturational processes and the facilitating environment* (pp. 37–55). International Universities Press.

Wittgenstein, L. (2001). *Tractatus logico-philosophicus.* Routledge.

Wong, P. (2012). The positive psychology of meaning and spirituality: Selected papers from meaning conferences. Purpose Research.

Yaden, D., Kaufman, B. Hyde, E., Chirico, A., Gaggioli, A. Zhang, J., & Keltner, D. (2018): The development of the Awe Experience Scale (AWE-S): A multifactorial measure for a complex emotion, *The Journal of Positive Psychology.* https://doi.org/10.1080/17439760.2018.1484940

Yerkes, R.M., & Dodson, J.D. (1908). The relation of strength of stimulus to rapidity of habit-formation. *Journal of Comparative Neurology and Psychology*, *18*(5), 459–482.

Zinn, H. (2003). *A peoples' history of the United States: 1492—present.* Harper-Perennial.

Index

Author Bio

Kirk J. Schneider, PhD, is a leading spokesperson for contemporary existential-humanistic and existential-integrative psychology. Dr. Schneider was a 2022 Candidate for President of the American Psychological Association (APA), a cofounder and current president of the Existential-Humanistic Institute (an award-winning psychotherapy training center), and a two-term Member of the Council of Representatives of the APA. He is also past president (2015-2016) of the Society for Humanistic Psychology (Division 32) of the APA, recent past editor of the *Journal of Humanistic Psychology* (2005-2012), a founder and frequent presenter/facilitator of the bridge-building dialogue approach the Experiential Democracy Dialogue, and a trained moderator for the conflict mediation group Braver Angels. Dr. Schneider is also an adjunct faculty member at Saybrook University and Teachers College, Columbia University and an Honorary Member of the Society for Existential Analysis of the UK and the East European Association for Existential Therapy. He received the Rollo May Award for "outstanding and independent contributions" to the field of humanistic psychology from the Society for Humanistic Psychology and is a Fellow of seven Divisions of the APA (5, 9, 32, 42, 12, 29, & 24). His work on existential-integrative psychotherapy has been featured in a special issue of the *Journal of Psychotherapy Integration* (March, 2016), as well as *The Wiley World Handbook of Existential Therapy* and the APA's forthcoming *Handbook of Psychotherapy*. Dr. Schneider has published over 200 articles, interviews, and chapters and has authored or edited 14 books, including *The Paradoxical Self, Horror and the Holy, Rediscovery of Awe, Awakening to Awe, The Spirituality of Awe, The Polarized Mind, The Handbook of Humanistic Psychology, Existential-Humanistic Therapy, Existential-Integrative Psychotherapy, The Wiley World Handbook of Existential Therapy,* and *The Depolarizing of America: A Guidebook for Social Healing.* Dr. Schneider's work has been featured in *Scientific American,* the *New York Times, USA Today, The Guardian, Vanity Fair, Forbes Health, Psychology Today, BBC World News,* and many other health and psychology outlets. For more information on Dr. Schneider's work visit https://kirkjschneider.com.

CPSIA information can be obtained
at www.ICGtesting.com
Printed in the USA
JSHW011423291222
35306JS00006B/182